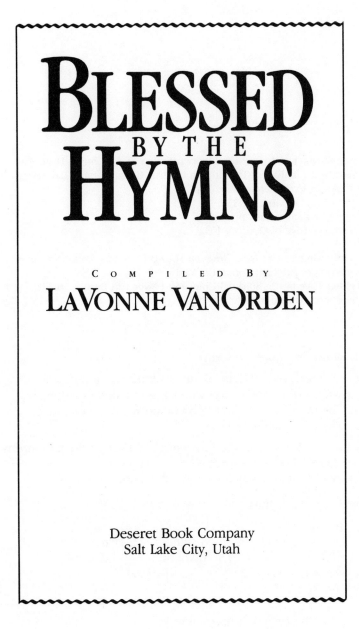

BLESSED
BY THE
HYMNS

COMPILED BY

LAVONNE VANORDEN

Deseret Book Company
Salt Lake City, Utah

The following articles are used by permission of the Church Historical
Department Archives of The Church of Jesus Christ of Latter-day Saints:
"It Was a Little Bit Remarkable," pp. 48-49;
"I Am a Child of God," p. 139;
"A Song Awakened Me," pp. 145-46;
"Prayer and Love of God," p. 153.

The following articles from *Brigham Young University Studies* reprinted by
permission of Brigham Young University:
"Welded Together in Spiritual Unity and Power and Beauty," p. 70;
"The Song Changed My Life," p. 160.

©1989 Deseret Book Company

All rights reserved. No part of this book may be reproduced
in any form or by any means without permission in writing
from the publisher, Deseret Book Company, P.O. Box 30178,
Salt Lake City, Utah 84130.

Deseret Book is a registered trademark of Deseret Book Company.

Library of Congress Cataloging-in-Publication Data

Blessed by the hymns.

    Includes index.
    1. Christian life—Mormon authors. 2. Hymns—History
and criticism. I. VanOrden, LaVonne.
BX8656.B63   1989   245'.21   88-33461
ISBN 0-87579-208-1

Printed in the United States of America
10   9   8   7   6   5   4   3   2

Be filled with the Spirit; speaking to yourselves in psalms and hymns and spiritual songs, singing and making melody in your heart to the Lord. (Ephesians 5:18-19.)

Contents

Preface

Ever since we shouted for joy in our pre-earth life (see Job 38:7), singing has been an important part of the Latter-day Saint heritage. The scriptures are replete with stories of the children of God singing for comfort, support, inspiration, and as expressions of worship and joy.

Moses and the children of Israel sang praises to the Lord for their deliverance from Pharaoh: "Then sang Moses and the children of Israel this song unto the Lord, and spake, saying, I will sing unto the Lord, for he hath triumphed gloriously." (Ex. 15:1.)

"And David spake unto the Lord the words of this song in the day that the Lord had delivered him out of the hand of all his enemies, and out of the hand of Saul." (2 Sam. 22:1.)

"And at midnight Paul and Silas prayed, and sang praises unto God: and the prisoners heard them." (Acts 16:25.)

And especially, the Lord Jesus Christ prepared for his ultimate sacrifice by singing a hymn. "And when they had sung an hymn, they went out into the mount of Olives." (Matt. 26:30.)

In our own dispensation the Prophet Joseph Smith, in the last moments before his martyrdom, found comfort in a hymn. The pioneer Saints in their trek westward often sang as they traveled.

Our prophets and General Authorities have shared their love of the hymns and the impact they have had on their own lives. Many have given sermons using the hymns as a means of teaching the gospel. "Sometimes I feel that we get nearer to the Lord through music than perhaps through any other thing except prayer," said President J. Reuben Clark. (See Conference Report, October 1936, p. 111.)

Although all good music can have a powerful effect on us, one kind of music, the hymn, has a unique influence that goes beyond music as an art. As the scriptures are to great literature, so are the hymns to great music. Elder Boyd K. Packer has said: "We are losing a powerful, spiritual force when we let the hymns of the Restoration fade from use. Classical music will not suffice. Other good music is not a substitute. Our indifference to the music of the Restoration is an indication that we do not understand the part it plays in spirituality." (Boyd K. Packer, General Authorities training meeting, 2 November 1983, p. 25; used by permission.)

Many people have been blessed by the hymns. Lives have been touched as hymns have brought about conversion or increased testimony. Hymns have given comfort, courage, or strength by opening communication through the spirit. The Lord has said that "the song of the righteous is a prayer unto me." (D&C 25:12.) Hymns, then, can be another form of communication with our Father in heaven. While we often think of singing hymns in church as a form of worship, praise, or supplication, we may not have realized that, like prayer, such communication can go in both directions: not only *from* us as an expression of praise, gratitude, worship, or pleading; but also *to* us as inspiration, guidance, comfort, or knowledge.

In these challenging days when evil influences are encroaching in our own lives and those of our children, and permeating even the sanctuary of our homes, who would not grasp at every available opportunity to marshall the forces for good? If there were a spiritual force that could be used to help strengthen and fortify our children in righteousness, would we not be eager to obtain it? If we were aware of an additional channel of communication with our Heavenly Father like unto prayer, would we ignore it?

There is such a force. There is such a channel. The stories in this book illustrate the spiritual power found in the hymns of the Restoration. It is available to all, regardless of musical ability or training. Just as prayer is not limited to the verbally articulate, neither is hymn experience limited to the musically articulate. Few of these recorded experiences were had by musicians. Some did not even involve music, but only the words of a hymn.

Read these stories for inspiration. Use them in Family Home

Evenings. Include them in Church lessons and talks. The hymns are not just for musicians nor are they just for singing. Let them become a powerful, spiritual force in the lives of all Latter-day Saints so that their lives, too, can be blessed by the hymns.

These accounts were gathered from books, periodicals, talks, newspapers, and personal acquaintances of the author. As much as possible they have been quoted as they were originally given — either as first-person accounts or told about someone by another person. In some cases they have been edited to include just the facts pertinent to the hymn story. In all cases, editorial comments by the author are given in italics.

The author gratefully acknowledges the encouragement and help which were given by Elder Yoshihiko Kikuchi and reference librarian Anna Mae Robison. And especially the continued and loving support of her husband, Richard.

ONE

FINDING COMFORT
THROUGH HYMNS

There are . . . many exquisite poems we sing in our services and homes. They are the source of light and comfort to many thousands, for where all else may fail, the hymn will bring comfort and trust in life and God. (Levi Edgar Young, "Our Hymns," Improvement Era, *June 1914, p. 759; used by permission.)*

REX D. PINEGAR
Did You Think to Pray?

IN 1943, I MET WITH AN ACCIDENT where I was seriously burned; an explosion that took my eyesight. On that evening as I lay on the operating table and Dr. Moody from Spanish Fork was trying to piece me back together, I asked for a blessing. Dr. Moody permitted my father to come in the operating room where the doctor anointed me and my father gave me a blessing. In that blessing, my father said, "Now Rex, if you will have faith, the Lord will make you whole." When he said that, into my mind came the words of this hymn,

> Ere you left your room this morning,
> Did you think to pray? . . .
> Oh, how praying rests the weary!
> Prayer will change the night to day.[1]

As I thought upon those words and upon my own condition, I thought, if anyone needed the night changed to day, I did. And so this hymn was in my mind and I actually hummed the hymn for over two and a half hours while the doctor put me back together.

Since that time it has had a very special meaning in my life. As I have pondered about that over the years I have thought about what the Lord said about hymns. He said, "The song of the righteous is a prayer unto me." I appreciate very much the impact that the prayers through the hymns have on the Lord and his resulting blessings to us.

---

1. *Hymns of The Church of Jesus Christ of Latter-day Saints* (Salt Lake City: The Church of Jesus Christ of Latter-day Saints, 1985), no. 140. Hereafter cited as *Hymns, 1985.*

Minutes of quorum meeting, First Quorum of the Seventy, 23 May 1985; used by permission.

MARION D. HANKS
I Began to Sing a Song

ONE NIGHT IN THE SOUTH PACIFIC, my wife and I were riding in the back of a very old minibus whose driver was cautiously guiding it through the flooded streets of Papeete on the island of Tahiti. Water was leaking into the bus as the heavens poured out great sheets of rain that were too much for the old roof and the cracked windows and the ancient windshield wipers. Fumes were seeping from cracked exhaust pipes up through the floor of the bus, and none of us were very comfortable. Some of the passengers became a little sick to their stomachs and worried about getting back to the hotel. We passed many stalled cars in streets that looked more like rivers than roads.

Everyone riding in the bus was attending a conference of South Sea mission presidents. There were leaders from Fiji, Samoa, Tonga, Hawaii, and Tahiti, plus some local priesthood leaders and visitors from Utah. Instead of just sitting there worrying, someone began to sing, and everyone quickly joined in. We sang well-known hymns and old familiar songs for a while. I began to sing a song I learned in Primary as a little boy: "Oh we are the boy trail builders, out west where the sunsets glow. . . . "

To my great surprise almost everyone in the bus knew the song. Many of them had grown up in the islands and had lived there all their lives, but when we started to sing Primary songs, everyone knew them and joined in.

Then we finished our songs by singing tenderly and lovingly, "I Am a Child of God." There weren't many people on the streets that rainy night, but those who were, and the bus driver, were at first curious about us and then respectful as they heard us singing through the storm.

"Friend to Friend," *Friend,* August 1978, pp. 8-9; used by permission.

4

YOSHIHIKO KIKUCHI

The Upper Room

Recently, while in Jerusalem, we visited the Upper Room where it is said the Savior, with his disciples, celebrated the Passover with the last supper in his mortal life. As we stood pondering, Sister Barbara Smith came to my side and asked, "Brother Kikuchi, do you think you could sing a song for us?" I began,

As I have loved you, Love one another.
This new commandment: Love one another.

A strong, peaceful, and very comforting spirit overwhelmed me. I just couldn't sing anymore. I stopped and tried three more times but I just couldn't go further. "I can't, I can't!" I said and I began to cry. All of us in the room cried like little children.

Then Sister Cheryl Blanchard came to my side. "Brother Kikuchi," she said. "I'm going to help you. Let's sing together." She began singing but it was no use. I could not sing because a strong, beautiful, and profound power just overwhelmed my whole soul and body and I started to tremble. I felt unworthy to come to sit at that sacred table. As I thought of that sacred and special hour when the Savior was sharing this greatest commandment with his disciples, I saw a little Japanese boy sticking his head into the door of the chamber, observing with a trembling heart the beautiful Savior and his disciples. I felt the sweetness of the deep, profound love of the Savior although, as a little boy, I could not comprehend the deep meaning of what was taking place. I was crying for joy and happiness—I felt like John the Beloved, squeezing into the bosom of the Holy One of Israel, the Savior of the world. I know he knows how I feel about him deep inside my soul, but I wanted to tell him how much I love Him and want to follow his beautiful teachings. I recommitted myself to help establish his beautiful kingdom on this earth.

When I came back to consciousness, Cheryl was still singing and this time I followed her. We all sang that beautiful song three times there in that chamber.

> As I have loved you, Love one another.
> This new commandment: Love one another.
> By this shall men know Ye are my disciples,
> If ye have love One to another.[1]

We were all touched as we felt the presence of his glorious spirit. What a beautiful, wonderful day that was!

---

1. *Hymns,* 1985, no. 308.

Unpublished; used by permission.

YOSHIHIKO KIKUCHI
I'll Go Where You Want Me to Go

O<small>N A RECENT VISIT TO THE HOLY LAND</small>, I was privileged to take a boat ride across the Sea of Galilee, from Tiberias to Capernaum. As we started across the sea on a trip that would take about fifty-five minutes, the Sea of Galilee itself was just like a mirror—beautiful and calm, with no wind. . . . It is such a beautiful, beautiful place. . . .

As we went along, I wanted to be alone from everyone to meditate—to think how this is where the Savior spent most of his time, right here around the shore of this beautiful sea. As I sat at the head of the boat with closed eyes, I could almost envision the many countless, beautiful, sacred, unforgettable, and sweet ministries of our Savior. I thanked God that I could come to this Holy Land where Jesus walked. A very special feeling came over me. In my mind, I was singing one song, "I'll Go Where You Want Me to Go."

It may not be on the mountain height
Or over the stormy sea,
It may not be at the battle's front
My Lord will have need of me.
But if, by the still, small voice he calls
To paths that I do not know,
I'll answer, dear Lord, with my hand in thine:
I'll go where you want me to go.
I'll go where you want me to go, dear Lord,
Over mountain or plain or sea;
I'll say what you want me to say, dear Lord;
I'll be what you want me to be.[1]

I noticed tears streaming down my face while I was humming this song and I felt the same overwhelming feeling I felt

---

1. *Hymns,* 1985, no. 270.

7

at the time President Spencer W. Kimball extended the call to me to serve as one of the General Authorities of His Church. "The Lord has called you to serve as one of the General Authorities of His Church! Would you accept this call?" At first, I couldn't accept. But, after a struggle with myself, I did accept. At that time, the thought came to me, "I'll go where you want me to go, dear Lord." On this boat on the Sea of Galilee, I felt once again a reassurance from the Lord that my call had come directly from Him. And my response was, "Dear Lord, with my hand in thine."

I felt the Spirit of the Lord touch my heart so much. Even now, as I remember that moment on the boat on the Sea of Galilee, I cannot stop my tears. I really want to be committed to this work of the Lord. I want to tell Him in my heart, "I will go where you want me to go. I will go where you go, dear Lord, over the mountains or plains or sea." When I said that to myself on the boat on the beautiful day, my whole body chilled and I felt the Spirit of the Lord come upon me and I felt the closeness of my Savior.

Unpublished; used by permission.

MELVIN J. BALLARD
Words of Comfort

YOUNG ELDER MELVIN J. BALLARD WAS having a difficult time getting to sleep. His mission was just months old, but the cacophony of emotion that surged within him indicated he was ready for it to be over.

He had been called on a special mission to several large cities in the eastern United States, and had been serving with Elders B. H. Roberts and George D. Pyper. The three missionaries had been sent out together, but now Elders Roberts and Pyper were being sent home. Elder Ballard, the youngest of the three and the most eager to return home, was being reassigned as a traveling elder in the northern states.

"Never had I felt such emotional distress," Elder Ballard said. "I wept through much of the night, not because I begrudged my service to the Lord, but because I so missed Martha." Martha, his bride, to whom he had been married just three weeks before receiving his mission call, was expecting their first child. His longing to be with her overwhelmed him.

But when temptation from the forces of evil began to enshroud him, he turned to the Lord for help. After a prayer for peace and strength, he began to read from a little book of poetry. He came upon some words written by Mary Brown that offered the comfort he sought:

> It may not be on the mountain height
> Or over the stormy sea,
> It may not be at the battle's front
> My Lord will have need of me.
> But if, by a still, small voice he calls
> To paths that I do not know,
> I'll answer, dear Lord, with my hand in thine:
> I'll go where you want me to go.[1]

---

1. *Hymns*, 1985, no. 270.

"I found in those words the assurance I needed," he said. "I resolved at that time to place my trust in God, and to go where He wanted me to go."

After Carrie E. Rounsefell set the poem to music, Elder Ballard, as a member of the Council of the Twelve, often sang the hymn to congregations he met with in his travels throughout the Church.

Joseph Walker "Words of Comfort," *Church News,* 28 August 1983, p. 16.

LOUISETTE CASTONGUAY
Tears Started Flowing

SIX MONTHS AFTER I HAD BEEN BAPTIZED, I had an impressive calling and was bending over backward to do things the way leaders would want. . . . Then I was released. I was devastated. It was tough for me. I almost stayed home that next Sunday. But I went and one of the hymns during sacrament meeting was "It May Not Be on the Mountain Height" ("I'll Go Where You Want Me to Go").

The tears started flowing again, as they had all week, but these were no longer tears of self-pity. They were tears of release to my Heavenly Father. I realized that perhaps He needed me elsewhere. Now the path was opened for me to pray about the situation in complete openness.

My answer was that I was supposed to be released at that time, according to the Lord's will. . . . Now, when I wonder at the judgment of people over me, I hum:

> It may not be on the mountain height
> Or over the stormy sea,
> It may not be at the battle's front
> My Lord will have need of me. . . .
> I'll go where you want me to go, dear Lord, . . .
> I'll be what you want me to be.[1]

I know the callings of the Church are by revelation, to help each individual grow, and to help the Church itself grow. I learned that I need to put myself at the Lord's disposal, not man's, and that He will use me . . . to accomplish that which is most needed of me at the time.

---

1. *Hymns,* 1985, no. 270.

"Hymns Bring Peace, Strength to Those in Need of Reassurance," *Church News,* 11 August 1985, p. 14.

GEORGE CARELESS
Though Deep'ning Trials Throng Your Way

THE TUNE TO [THE] SONG IS AMONG THE best creations of the harmonious pen of George Careless, one of the most renowned composers of the Church. As the pen of Eliza R. Snow fashioned her hymn amidst the tribulations of the people, so, at a later date, George Careless composed the tune while under physical distress. He was very ill and needed encouragement—something to dispel his fears and raise him from the state of despondency into which he felt himself drifting. From searching the Scriptures he turned to his loved hymn book to which he had already contributed many notable tunes.

"Addie," he called to his eleven-year-old daughter, "bring me the hymn book." She brought it to him. After scanning its pages for a few minutes he found what he was searching for— what his physical body as well as his spirit required. It was Eliza R. Snow's hymn, "Though Deep'ning Trials Throng Your Way."[1] It gave him courage to fight his bodily ills and the faith that soon raised him from his bed of affliction. At the same time it inspired the muse that enabled him to pen one of the noblest of his compositions—one which, united with Eliza R. Snow's comforting poem, is among the most popular numbers in our Church hymnody.

---

1. At that time, hymn texts were printed in the hymnbook without music.

George D. Pyper, *Stories of Latter-day Saint Hymns* (Salt Lake City: Deseret News Press, 1939), pp. 140-41.

NICHOLAS G. SMITH
The Singing Moved Him Deeply

BEING THE SON OF Apostle John Henry Smith did not auto-matically give Elder Nicholas Smith[1] a knowledge that the gos-pel was true. In fact, he records that when he received a mission call to the Netherlands in 1902, he did not have a testimony. Perhaps that is the very reason he accepted the call. His wise father had counseled him, "Now, son, in respect to the gospel, if you want to have a testimony about any part of it, live that part of it and you will get your testimony. . . . Do not accept it because I tell you it is true." (Romney, *The Gospel in Action*, p. 223.)

After beginning his mission, Nicholas became skeptical and bitter — refusing to pray, complaining about the difficult con-ditions, rejecting the unfamiliar food offered him by the Dutch Saints, and threatening to go home. His first Sunday in the Netherlands he would not attend the Church services which were held one floor below his apartment. During the meeting the congregation sang in Dutch a hymn called "In Our Lovely Deseret." The singing moved him deeply, and he fell to his knees and pleaded with the Lord for a knowledge of the truth and the strength to do His will. Both blessings were granted, and Nicholas Smith became one of the most outstanding elders in the mission, baptizing thirty people and serving as president of the Amsterdam Conference.

---

1. Nicholas G. Smith was Acting Patriarch to the Church from 1932 to 1934 and Assistant to the Quorum of the Twelve from 1941 until his death in 1945.

Lawrence R. Flake, *Mighty Men of Zion* (Salt Lake City: Deseret Press, 1974), p. 320; used by permission.

ALICE WASHBURN
Still Singing by My Side

DURING THE LAST FEW YEARS OF my mother's life, my sisters and I took turns caring for her, and I learned to love and appreciate her more than ever before. What a dedicated, faithful mother, teacher, and example of living the gospel she was! When she passed away, I missed her greatly.

One Sunday several months later, I was sitting in sacrament meeting singing the hymn, "Do What Is Right." I suddenly heard my mother's voice clearly singing in my ear. I couldn't mistake the strong, clear voice that had sung so many songs near my side. As we started the second chorus, "Do what is right; let the consequence follow," my heart seemed to stop. I put my hands to my cheeks and looked around me. My husband, who sat at my side, hadn't heard anything; I could tell by looking at his face.

I was so overcome that I couldn't control my emotions. I covered my face as my pounding heart seemed to repeat, "Do what is right; let the consequence follow" — just that, nothing more. But I felt such a glorious feeling! My mother was counseling me to live righteously, at all costs.

Sometimes the right decisions still don't come easily, but this experience has strengthened my testimony. I will always remember feeling my mother's presence counseling me to stay firm in keeping the commandments of our Lord.

"Still Singing by My Side," *Ensign*, October 1986, p. 55; used by permission.

CONNEE GARRETT
Hold to the Rod

THERE ARE TIMES WHEN MUSIC CAN soothe a troubled soul, alleviate fears, move us to good works, and renew our reverence for things of the Spirit. A friend told me of an incident in her life when a few short lines of one hymn made a lasting impression. Her oldest daughter had just given birth to a beautiful baby boy, her first grandchild. Two weeks later, she received a frantic call: "Mom, come quick — the baby!" When she arrived at the small apartment, the baby was lying lifeless on the couch. He had been well when put to bed the night before, but from unknown causes had slept silently into death.

She felt that her heart would break, and her faith wavered as she cried, "Why, Lord, why?" Then, as if in answer, came to her mind the strains of

> Hold to the rod, the iron rod;
> 'Tis strong, and bright, and true.
> The iron rod is the word of God;
> 'Twill safely guide us through.[1]

She did hold to the rod, and saw her daughter's husband embrace the beautiful principle of life after death and join the Church. Her daughter and son-in-law are now united by a temple marriage and have that beautiful little spirit sealed to them, along with three other sons.

---

1. *Hymns*, 1985, no. 274.

"A Song of the Heart," *Ensign*, June 1982, p. 37; used by permission.

15

MELVA LEE WHEELWRIGHT
My First Night Alone

THE OPPRESSING SILENCE WAS MORE THAN I could bear. I tried to find company in a television news program, but the tinny, artificial sound of the old set seemed to compound my nervousness. It was my first night alone.

My husband and I had been married only six months. He had warned me that from time to time he would have to be away overnight, but I had pushed the thought deep into the back of my mind, not wanting such a day to come. I was terrified of being alone. I had been the victim of an attempted attack earlier in my life—at night—alone.

The television news began with scenes of accidents, tales of crime. Hardly comforting. The normal groans and creaks from our old house evoked visions of prowlers. I shut off the set and turned on several lights and began to pace restlessly from one room to another. Finally I realized that I couldn't face the next twenty-four hours in this frame of mind, so summoning what courage I could, I turned off the lights and went into the bedroom.

I sat on the bed and tried to get control of myself, and in desperation I cried out to the Lord to comfort me and bring peace to my frightened soul. Just as I finished my plea, I seemed to hear in my mind the strains of a simple melody, coming unbidden and at first unnoticed. But as the music continued, it captured my entire attention. It was a hymn, not a familiar one; in fact, I couldn't think of the title or the words.

I relaxed and listened intently as the hymn rang on through my heart until it broke into the final glorious stanza. At that point the words came into my mind with perfect clarity and conviction: "My noonday walks he will attend, And all my silent midnight hours defend."[1]

---

1. *Hymns,* 1985, no. 109.

In this, my own silent midnight hour, the melody faded away, but I continued to ponder those words of comfort. As I did so, my soul was filled from the center outward with a wave of sweet warmth. I knew my prayer had been answered. I rested well that night, knowing that the Lord, our Shepherd, loves all his children, and that I am one of them.

"My First Night Alone," *Ensign,* January 1976, p. 48; used by permission.

VERA N. FORSYTH
Music Brought Me Comfort

W E WERE TWO THOUSAND MILES AWAY from our home in Alberta, Canada, visiting our daughter's family. My husband, who had sprained his ankle the evening we arrived, was in the hospital with a blood clot. He lay in a bed, immobilized, with an IV in his arm.

As I left his room after my first visit, I felt a little blue. I was in an unfamiliar place, lonely and worried about the responsibilities we had waiting for us at home.

Our daughter wanted some things for the baby, so we stopped at a department store. Because I didn't feel like shopping, I walked over to a clerk demonstrating a beautiful electric organ.

"Do you play?" he asked.

"Only a little," I replied.

"Sit down and try it then." I sat and softly played . . . "How Great Thou Art." Suddenly I heard a lady singing along with me. Her rich soprano and the sound of the organ had attracted people from all over the store. The clerk pushed button after button until the organ sounded like a whole orchestra. Suddenly I felt strong. The words of the song brought me a message. We would get home safely, everything would be all right. The blessing of the music and words at that time seemed heaven-sent to lift me up and I thanked my Father in Heaven for the power of sacred music.

"Music Brought Me Comfort," *Ensign*, February 1985, p. 55; used by permission.

KATHY WILCOX
Tornado

DURING THE RETURN JOURNEY [from an area conference in Wisconsin], we ran into a severe thunderstorm and I was separated from my husband['s truck] for ten minutes due to poor visibility. [The children and I] pulled to the highway shoulder to ask our Heavenly Father to help us know which turn to take. Within five minutes we were right behind my husband again. But the storm had not lessened, and in the blinding rain we were again separated. . . . We were now fairly isolated, traveling in unfamiliar territory, and into a storm which was rapidly getting worse. . . .

The little ones were worried despite my reassurances that we would be safe. . . . Their fears were only magnified when people told us there were tornado warnings coming from the direction we were headed and we were entirely foolish to travel this road any further.

Amid the children's tearful comments, we offered another prayer. . . . Then we continued on our way, and I decided we should start singing. We began with light-hearted fun songs and folk tunes, and finally gospel hymns. Just a few minutes after beginning the hymns a beautiful peace permeated the car, and the children one by one fell into restful sleep.

The peace was wonderful as I continued to sing, noticing all the while that I was driving toward the blackest storm I had ever seen. I felt the whispering of the Spirit to continue straight ahead. The air seemed very quiet, and the only sounds inside the car were my own beating heart and the children's quiet breathing. Never have I felt such silence. Then suddenly the blackness was all around us, and blinding rain and winds of terrible force struck the car. I gasped. Then I heard a resounding heavenly choir repeating these familiar lines:

When dark clouds of trouble hang o'er us
And threaten our peace to destroy,

19

There is hope smiling brightly before us,
And we know that deliv'rance is nigh.
We doubt not the Lord nor his goodness.
We've proved him in days that are past.
The wicked who fight against Zion
Will surely be smitten at last.[1]

. . . We did make it home safely. Although a tornado had struck, tearing out a small trailer park and ravaging everything in its path, by news reports we determined that my husband was ahead of it by only a few minutes, and I would have been in its center had the Spirit not directed me to another road. I was grateful for the sure knowledge I gained that our Father does know and love his children, that he sees the entire road map and will safely guide us to our destination if we but heed him.

---

1. *Hymns,* 1985, no. 19.

"Tornado," *Ensign,* June 1981, p. 71; used by permission.

RICHARD RUST
Hymn of Comfort

I was going through an emotional crisis associated with a divorce. I was ill-prepared for this sudden change in my life.... "You've got to pull yourself out of this slump," [my mother] said. "This is something you can't change. You must accept it and go on with life. I'm sorry it happened. But you have the welfare of your son to think about, and when you're down it saddens him too." I knew she was right, but it was hard to focus my thoughts....

Tears came easily as I wrapped myself in self-pity. I couldn't see any end to this relentless suffering. I couldn't see a future, or any hope for better times. There seemed to be no one to turn to. All the people I talked to tried to offer me comfort, but it was no use. Their sympathy only brought out more emotion. The pressure seemed to build and intensify until I thought my sanity was going to vanish. At last I cried aloud in desperation, "God help me. Give me back my wife!"

I was not accustomed to praying, but I had come to a point where I knew of no other direction to turn. There was a time when I knew how to pray and was quite active in the Church, but somehow I had slipped away and was caught up in worldly ways.

Now something was happening, though. No sooner had I cried out than a wonderful feeling came over me. I can't describe it. It was just a feeling of power encompassing me, protecting me. And then words came to me, words and vaguely familiar notes of music, words of a hymn I had heard before, but in a different time of my life. I began to sing, and as I sang, every word fell into place:

> We thank thee, O God, for a prophet
> To guide us in these latter days.
> We thank thee for sending the gospel
> To lighten our minds with its rays.

21

We thank thee for every blessing
Bestowed by thy bounteous hand.
We feel it a pleasure to serve thee,
And love to obey thy command.

The verse came to me as clearly as if I had sung this hymn
every day of my life. Yet I know I had not sung or even thought
of it for over fifteen years. I sang it over and over, louder; I
didn't care if anyone heard me. To me it was a healing force,
and it gave me comfort.

When dark clouds of trouble hang o'er us
And threaten our peace to destroy,
There is hope smiling brightly before us,
And we know that deliv'rance is nigh.
We doubt not the Lord nor his goodness,
We've proved him in days that are past. . . .
We'll sing of his goodness and mercy.
We'll praise him by day and by night,
Rejoice in his glorious gospel,
And bask in its life-giving light.[1]

It was my Heavenly Father's answer to my plea, and I shall
never forget the words and the spirit that permeated my soul
as I sang the words and contemplated their meaning.

In the months that followed, I called upon my Heavenly
Father many times to help me through the trials of that difficult
time, and he was always there. I learned something from that
experience. There is someone you can turn to in time of need.
He didn't chastise, ridicule, or upbraid me for ignoring him
for so many years. He simply let me know that he was there
all the time, and all I had to do was call. . . .

Thank God for his goodness and mercy.

---

1. *Hymns*, 1985, no. 19.

"Hymn of Comfort," *Ensign*, September 1983, pp. 63-64; used by permission.

COLLEEN C. EVANS
Fear Not, for the Lord Is on Our Side

SEVERAL YEARS AGO WE WERE DRIVING to Idaho from Florida where we had lived for some time. Behind us was our thirty-foot mobile home full of furniture. Although it was still early spring we were unprepared for the snow we found in the mountains of Southern Idaho. As we started to climb, something slipped and one of the rear wheels of the trailer slid off the edge of the road. Fortunately, we were balanced so we didn't slide down the mountain, but we couldn't move. Just as we got out to assess the situation, a big highway sanding truck came along. The driver stopped, seeing that we were in a desperate situation. He wasn't authorized to help us, he said, but because he could see that we couldn't help ourselves he would do what he could.

As he attached a chain to the front of our car to pull us back onto the road, he started whistling. Immediately the words to the tune he was whistling flashed into my mind: "Fear not, for the Lord is on our side." Then, I just relaxed. I knew that I need not fear, for the Lord was there and we would be rescued. I also realized that we were back in Mormon country and it felt good to hear a Mormon hymn from a truck driver who just happened to come along.

Unpublished; used by permission.

23

Paul Sutorius
Peace—If Not Plenty—Here Abides

I TURNED OFF THE LIGHTS IN THE already deserted office and locked the back door behind me. A cold February blast met me as I walked toward the only car left in the parking lot. It was [an old] sports coupe, with the backseat taken out to accommodate all our little kids. . . . The car started on the first try and I eased . . . out into the steady stream of evening traffic. . . .

I had to face facts. No amount of positive thinking or vain hopes could make them go away. The day I had most dreaded, and hoped would never come, had arrived. The business had run its course. And although I had realized for some time that I was "riding a dead horse," I had hoped it would revive. It hadn't. I was now financially finished and faced with the burden of carrying the carcass around with me for many years. . . .

The two-lane road was thick darkness behind me. "I'm sure there are others in those passing cars who share this same sickening feeling," I thought. "There must be others like me, who are going home to tell their families that tomorrow will be different—that changes are coming, tightening up—maybe embarrassment." The family soon would know firsthand that along with the dream of success and prosperity comes the possibility of failure and loss. Whatever the reasons or rationale, they had to accept with me that I'd entered the race and lost.

As my mind turned again to the cars and trucks flowing past me into the night, I thought how easy it would be to turn the wheel ever so slightly and meet one of those huge, freight-laden semi trucks head on. . . . It might be a painless "accident" and the thought of possible insurance money for my family made it briefly tempting. Then thoughts of eternal ramifications, not to mention funerals, tear-filled eyes, and long times of loneliness overwhelmed me, and I banished the ugly plan from my mind. . . .

And now, having shut the door to my office one last time, I followed the familiar patterns of rights and lefts that would bring me home. I slowed as I approached our rented home. . . . I shut off the engine and lights and coasted to the curb across the street. It was time for mustering up. Time to get complete control of myself and forget the day. . . .

Then from across the street I began to hear the sounds of our old upright piano. My wife often gathered the children around the piano before dinner and had them sing with her until daddy got home. This little practice not only kept their minds off their stomachs, but established a real atmosphere of love and unity. The sounds of their high, sweet voices drifted across the street:

> There is beauty all around
> When there's love at home;
> There is joy in ev'ry sound
> When there's love at home.
> Peace and plenty here abide,
> Smiling sweet on ev'ry side.
> Time doth softly, sweetly glide
> When there's love at home.[1]

Tears were now flowing freely down my face. I began to count my blessings. I was still young; I had a wife who loved and supported me in all that I strived to do; I had lovely children, my living treasures, who needed and loved me too. And to sustain and cheer us all, we had a common belief in a God whom we gratefully called Father. I was rich in the things that really mattered. For now, I would take no thought for the morrow. I owed my loved ones a smile at the end of the day, a cheerful greeting, a hug and a kiss. They deserved a reassuring attitude, one that said we *could* and *would* make it. The knowledge I had of the Savior's reality made anything possible.

---

1. *Hymns,* 1985, no. 294.

"Peace — If Not Plenty — Here Abides," *Ensign,* February 1983, pp. 55-56; used by permission.

LaVonne VanOrden
Cast Thy Burden upon the Lord

THERE WAS A TIME IN MY LIFE WHEN life's problems seemed almost too much to bear. Though I was active in the Church and felt I was trying to live the gospel, it seemed as though my pleadings to the Lord were unanswered.

One day in Relief Society, the opening hymn was "Cast Thy Burden upon the Lord," which had always been one of my favorites. However, that day, because of the severe anguish I had been experiencing over my personal problems and my inability to receive the comfort, guidance, or understanding I was seeking in order to cope with them, I felt doubtful, almost cynical, as we sang:

> Cast thy burden upon the Lord,
> And he shall sustain thee.
> He never will suffer the righteous to fall.
> He is at thy right hand.[1]

Upon returning from Relief Society that morning, I once again knelt beside my bed and approached my Father in Heaven. I included in my prayer that day the reminder that He had promised that if we would cast our burdens upon Him, He would surely sustain us, yet it had seemed that my petitions had been in vain. As I knelt there reaching longingly for some reassurance that my prayers had been heard, I felt strong arms around me. Though there was no other mortal in the room with me that day, I actually felt the comfort of being cradled in the arms of my Heavenly Father. I knew for a certainty that:

> Thy mercy, Lord, is great And far above the heav'ns.
> Let none be made ashamed That wait upon thee.

---

1. *Hymns,* 1985, no. 110.

Unpublished; used by permission.

JERRY BORROWMAN
You're the Future of the World

IT WAS COLD, DARK, AND DAMP, and as we pulled up in front of the small Catholic nursing home, our thoughts were centered more on hot chocolate and popcorn than on Christmas caroling. We missionaries had spent a wonderful day singing in hospitals and nursing homes throughout southern Dallas. But now it was late, and our voices were tired. We were glad to arrive at the last stop of the day.

Inside it smelled musty. We huddled for a few minutes in one corner of the foyer while the Catholic sisters brought their patients in wheelchairs to hear us sing.

As we started the first carol, a remarkable thing happened. In spite of our hoarse throats, our singing sounded more clear and true than at any of the other performances we had given that day. A feeling of warmth enveloped us. We were filled with a sense of peace and reverence.

After we finished the last song, the nurses asked us to wait while they returned the patients to their rooms. A few minutes later, the sisters came back to thank us for coming. Sensing that they didn't want us to leave yet, we volunteered to sing one more song for them. Rather than a traditional carol, we softly sang:

> I know that my Redeemer lives.
> What comfort this sweet sentence gives!
> He lives, he lives, who once was dead.
> He lives, my everliving Head.
> He lives to bless me with his love.
> He lives to plead for me above.
> He lives my hungry soul to feed.
> He lives to bless in time of need. . . .
> He lives! All glory to his name!
> He lives, my Savior, still the same.

Oh, sweet the joy this sentence gives:
"I know that my Redeemer lives!"[1]

With tears in their eyes, the nuns, who were selflessly spending their lives serving others, rushed forward to thank us. One sister, the supervisor of the others, took my hands in hers and said, "You're the future of the world, do you realize that? You young men are the future of the world!"

As a young missionary, I sensed her sincerity — and the new hope and faith we had brought into her life. For a moment our differences disappeared, and we all received a witness, borne by the Spirit of God, that Jesus Christ does indeed live.

1. *Hymns,* 1985, no. 136.

"You're the Future of the World," *Ensign,* December 1985, p. 66; used by permission.

KATHRYN WOUDEN
The Old Man Who Sang

I RUSHED TO THE TIME CLOCK, found my card, and quickly punched it in. . . . I worked as an evening receptionist at one of the larger convalescent centers for the elderly in Salt Lake City, Utah. As I walked to my desk, I heard a voice singing "There's Sunshine in My Soul Today." The voice was bellowing the song out at the top of its lungs. Curious, I followed the sound of the voice. At the end of one of the corridors, I found a husky old man sitting up in his bed. The cords on his neck stood out with the strain of singing.

"Hello!" he called out to me cheerfully. He didn't seem surprised to see me standing there. He just grinned brightly at me. The windows were wide open. The air and sunshine poured in. It seemed to be one of the most cheerful rooms that I had ever been in, yet it was similar to all of the other rooms in the building.

"I heard you singing," I remarked to him.

"Good!" He nodded his head courteously at me. "I sing because it makes me happy!"

As duties awaited me at my desk, I said good-bye to him. As I went down the hall, I heard him singing "High on the Mountain Top" as if he were yodeling it from the hilltops. For the rest of the evening I found myself humming, "High on the mountain top. . . ."

The next day I managed to arrive a few minutes early. Again, I heard the cheerful voice singing. Irresistibly pulled, I went down to his room. "Well, hello, young lady!" His eyes and toothless smile welcomed me as if I were a queen. I greeted him and asked if I could listen to him sing. "Sure!" He invited me to sit down on the only chair in the room. He sang through all the verses of "How Firm a Foundation." His off-key voice charmed me. I asked him if he knew "The World Has Need

29

of Willing Men." This was a favorite song of mine. I had taught it to my youngest brother when he was just four.

Not only did he sing it for me, but he sang it with such force that I couldn't help but join him and sing too. I caught his enthusiasm and sang much louder than I normally would. A nurse passed by and glanced at us curiously. As I left, I asked him when he had taken time to memorize all the hymns. "Oh, that's easy!" He clapped his hands together. "I memorized them as I sang them in church. Once I knew them, I never opened the hymn book again!" I made a resolve to do the same.

It became regular routine to stop in at his room before I went down to my desk. He always greeted me brightly. I found myself humming Church hymns between my classes at the university.

Christmastime came and my classes were over for three weeks. As I had made arrangements with someone to take my place at work during that time, I was free to go home and visit my family in Ephraim, Utah. Before I left, however, I stopped in to see the old man. We sang through countless Christmas carols together. I was more in the Christmas spirit than I had ever been before. I left him singing a rousing version of "Silent Night."

As I walked back down the corridor, I passed a nurse who frowned at me. I didn't recall seeing her before. I puzzled about it for a minute and then shrugged it off. I was too happy to let a frown bother me. Later, I found out that she had just recently been hired as the head nurse.

Christmas vacation, as always, flew by too fast for me. . . . When I stepped through the doors at the convalescent center to go back to work, I expected to hear a cheerful voice booming out some song down the hall. As I punched in my time card at the time clock, I cocked my ear for his voice. All I could hear was the confusion of a few televisions tuned to different stations and conversation of a few patients who were sitting near me in the hallway. "He's probably asleep," I said to myself. But, to reassure myself, I walked down to his room. I peeked in the door, expecting to see him curled up in bed sound asleep. However, he was sitting with his back supported by a few pillows. The windows were half shut and the curtains pulled. He sat listlessly in the half gloom.

Hearing my step, he slowly turned his head and saw me. He grinned the ghost of a smile. I was shocked. His wrinkled skin hung in loose pouches around his face as if he had lost a great amount of weight. "I . . . I thought you'd be singing," I stammered out. He shook his head and tears slid down his cheeks. "Can't sing anymore. Nurse said it bothered too many people." He looked at me earnestly. "I don't want to bother anyone. Singing just made me happy." There was a long pause as he thought. "No, I don't want to bother anyone," he repeated.

I blinked back tears as I walked over and took his hand. "Why don't we sing together right now?"

He looked at me anxiously, "Oh no, please don't. I don't think she would like it."

"Well, then," I said softly, "I'll sing. I'll sing so quietly that no one will hear me but you."

I softly sang the first song that came to me. I sang all the verses of "I Am a Child of God" for him. His wrinkled lips mouthed most of the words with me. After singing, I talked softly with him for a while and rubbed his brow. As I needed to get to my desk, I told him I would be back tomorrow. He called me when I had reached the door. I turned to look at him questioningly. His leathery cheeks wrinkled deeply as he gave me a smile. His eyes had a hint of their old sparkle.

As soon as I got out into the hall, I was fighting mad. I couldn't wait to find the nurse who had done this. Angry words were close to the surface of my thoughts.

I didn't have to search long. The new head nurse was waiting for me at the end of the hall. Before I could even say a word, she demanded, "Young lady, what were you doing there?" I explained that I worked at the center as a receptionist and that the old man was a friend of mine. I tried to go on and explain about his singing, but she cut me off. "Well, if you're the receptionist here, then go do your work. You have no right to be back here with the patients." She planted her feet in front of me and folded her chin firmly into her neck.

"I just wanted to tell you that you're making the old man

sick by not letting him sing! It makes him happy to sing!" I said this in a rush before she could stop me.

She thrust her face in front of mine. "The old man is dying from an incurable disease. *Not* from the reason you state." She checked her watch. "Now, if you're the evening receptionist, you're already fifteen minutes late. If you still want your job, I advise you to go immediately to your desk and leave this part of the building to me."

I walked through the building to my desk. I made a resolve to see the old man tomorrow regardless of the nurse. Even if I had to crawl through the window, I would go to him and sing for him until he was well enough to sing like he used to.

The next afternoon I arrived at work early so I could spend more time with the old man. I stepped cautiously into the center watching for the head nurse. There was no sign of her. I reached his room without having an encounter with her. Relieved, I turned to go into his room. The drapes and windows were wide open and sunshine spread through the room. The bed was tightly made and the floor appeared to be newly waxed. There was no sign of the old man or his personal possessions. I was filled with dread at the sight of the well-cleaned room. My footsteps dragged as I walked down to the nurse's station to inquire about him.

"Room 67?" She repeated after me. I nodded. The nurse aide then turned to a chart and examined it for a minute. She looked up at me. "He died last night about 2:00 A.M."

Tears blinded my vision as I stumbled down the hall to my desk. I wished with all my heart that I had done more for him. All I could think of was the smile he had given me before I had left him yesterday. It had been a grateful smile.

When I reached my desk, I laid my head down and cried helpless tears for the old man. The telephone rang. As I composed myself to answer it, I thought I could hear the faint echo of "There's Sunshine in My Soul Today." Suddenly I felt strongly that the old man would be singing at the top of his lungs today. Maybe I was hearing the faint echo of his voice from heaven. I smiled through my tears and started to softly hum the tune.

"The Old Man Who Sang," *New Era,* September 1978, pp. 40, 42; used by permission.

TWO

COME SINGING
UNTO ZION

Therefore the redeemed of the Lord shall return, and come with singing unto Zion; and everlasting joy shall be upon their head: they shall obtain gladness and joy; and sorrow and mourning shall flee away. (Isaiah 51:11.)

JOSEPH SMITH
A Christmas Serenade

*M*onday, *December 25, 1843*

This morning, about one o'clock, I was aroused by an English sister, Lettice Rushton, . . . accompanied by three of her sons, with their wives, and her two daughters, with their husbands, and several of her neighbors, singing, "Mortals awake! with angels join," &c., which caused a thrill of pleasure to run through my soul. All of my family and boarders arose to hear the serenade, and I felt to thank my Heavenly Father for their visit, and blessed them in the name of the Lord. They also visited my brother Hyrum, who was awakened from his sleep. He arose and went out of doors. He shook hands with and blessed each one of them in the name of the Lord, and said that he thought at first that a cohort of angels had come to visit him, it was such heavenly music to him.

History of the Church of Jesus Christ of Latter-day Saints, 6:134.

JOSEPH SMITH
A Poor Wayfaring Man of Grief

*On June 28, 1844, Joseph and Hyrum were impris-
oned in Carthage Jail along with Willard Richards and
John Taylor, both of the Quorum of the Twelve.*

W E ALL OF US FELT UNUSUALLY DULL AND languid, with a
remarkable depression of spirits. In consonance with those
feelings I sang a song, that had lately been introduced into
Nauvoo, entitled, 'A Poor Wayfaring Man of Grief, etc.'

"The song is pathetic, and the tune quite plaintive, and was
very much in accordance with our feelings at the time for our
spirits were all depressed, dull and gloomy and surcharged
with indefinite ominous forebodings." (John Taylor, *History of
the Church,* 7:101.)

The afternoon was sultry and hot. The four brethren sat
listlessly about the room with their coats off; and the windows
of the prison were open to receive such air as might be stirring.
Late in the afternoon Mr. Stigall, the jailor, came in and suggested that they would be safer in the cells. Joseph told him
that they would go in after supper. . . .

Hyrum Smith asked Elder Taylor to sing again, "A Poor
Wayfaring Man of Grief."

Elder Taylor: "Brother Hyrum, I do not feel like singing.

Hyrum: Oh, never mind: commence singing and you will
get the spirit of it."

Soon after finishing the song the second time, as he was
sitting at one of the front windows, Elder Taylor saw a number
of men, with painted faces, rushing round the corner of the
jail towards the stairs. . . .

How quickly disastrous things happened! Three minutes
after the attack was commenced upon the jail, Hyrum Smith
lay stretched upon the floor of the prison—dead; John Taylor
lay not far from him savagely wounded; the Prophet was lying

outside the jail by the old well curb—dead; the mob in consternation and disorder had fled...; the plighted faith of the state was broken, its honor trailed in the dust, and a stain of innocent blood affixed to its escutcheon that will remain a blot which time cannot efface.

B. H. Roberts, *A Comprehensive History of the Church of Jesus Christ of Latter-day Saints,* 2:283-84, 286-87.

ELIZA R. SNOW

The Glory of God Seemed to Rest on All

Many, yes many were the star and moonlight evenings, when, as we circled around the blazing fire and sang our hymns of devotion and songs of praise to Him who knows the secrets of all hearts—when with sublime union of hearts, the sound of united voices reverberated from hill to hill; and echoing through the silent expanse, apparently filled the vast concave above, while the glory of God seemed to rest on all around us.

On one of these soul-inspiring occasions—prompted by the spirit of Song, I wrote the following:

SONG OF THE DESERT

Beneath the cloud-topp'd mountain—
Beside the craggy bluff,
Where every dint of nature
Is wild and rude enough:
Upon the verdant meadow—
Upon the sun-burnt plain—
Upon the sandy hillock,
We waken music's strain.
Beneath the humble cedar,
And the green cotton-wood:
Beside the broad smooth river—
Beside the flowing spring—
Beside the limpid streamlet,
We often sit and sing.
Beneath the sparkling concave,
When stars in millions come
To cheer the weary strangers
And bid us feel at home.

Amid the cheering moon-light,
Fair Cynthia's mellow rays
In social groups we gather,
And join in songs of praise.
Cheer'd by the blaze of fire-light,
When evening shadows fall,
And when the darkness deepens
Around our spacious hall;
With true and warm emotion
To saintly bosoms given,
In strains of pure devotion
We praise the God of heaven.

Eliza R. Snow, An Immortal (Salt Lake City: Nicholas G. Morgan, Sr., Foundation, 1957), pp. 27-28.

JANE PASKET JUDD
I Would Like to Sing

My GREAT-GRANDMOTHER'S NAME IS Jane Pasket Judd. She belonged to the Church of England before she joined the Mormon Church.

My great-grandmother left England in June 1868, with her brother, John Pasket, and a company of saints on their way to America. They crossed the sea in a sailing vessel named "Constitution," and were six weeks on the sea. On arriving at Benton City, Iowa, they were met by teamsters with ox teams, who were to take them to Utah. Great-grandmother walked part of the way, but was taken sick with mountain fever and it was necessary for her to ride.

An old lady from the same village as my great-grandmother, rode in the wagon with her. This lady was taken sick with cholera. Great-grandmother was very kind to her and learned to love her. She continued to grow worse and one day when the company camped for dinner some quilts were laid on the grass for her to rest. Great-grandmother asked her if she could do anything for her and she said, "Yes, I would like to sing."

Grandmother asked her what she would like to sing and she replied, "Let us sing 'We Thank Thee, O God, for a Prophet.'" They sang together, and in a very short time the old lady died. Her name was Sister Clayfield. She was buried on the hillside on the Pioneer Trail.

The company did not travel farther that day. It was with aching hearts they left the lonely grave by the wayside.

Clair Wright, "I Would Like to Sing," *Children's Friend*, July 1941, p. 329; used by permission.

EZRA T. BENSON
A Song for a Lion

I RECALL VERY VIVIDLY AN EXPERIENCE told to me by my grandfather.

My great-grandfather, Apostle Ezra Taft Benson,[1] and his wife, and two little boys, George, seven, and Frank A., one, had come from Missouri to make their home in Cache Valley. Great-grandfather and some other men had to explore Cache Valley to find suitable places for other pioneers who were coming to live here.

Great-grandfather left great-grandmother with the boys in a rather sage-brush covered place. As they were sitting outside the covered wagon, about an hour after the men had gone, she heard a noise, and there was a big lion standing on its haunches about a hundred feet from where they were. It looked like it was ready to attack, so great-grandmother prayed in her heart and asked the Lord what to do. She was impressed to sing. This she did and the lion went away without harming her. Then she knelt down and thanked the Lord for saving the lives of herself and the children.

This was a great testimony to my great-grandmother and to Frank A. Benson, my grandfather, who was also present.

---

1. Ezra T. Benson, the great-grandfather of Ezra Taft Benson, thirteenth President of the Church, was one of the Twelve Apostles from 1846 until his death in 1869.

Margaret Benson, "A Song for a Lion," *Children's Friend*, July 1941, p. 308; used by permission.

CHARLES W. PENROSE

School Thy Feelings, O My Brother

School thy feelings, O my brother;
Train thy warm, impulsive soul.
Do not its emotions smother,
But let wisdom's voice control.[1]

[This] hymn was written by President Charles W. Penrose, missionary, General Authority and poet and one of the most prolific speakers of the Church. The hymn was written... shortly before President Penrose was to leave England for the United States in 1861 after serving a ten-year mission. As President Penrose was to tell the congregation in a sacrament meeting a few years later, the verses were written to himself and for "giving a little counsel to myself." ... He said: "This was written under peculiar circumstances just before I left England, after having traveled over ten years in the ministry. A sort of quiet slander had been circulated concerning me in Birmingham by an elder from Zion and it had cut me to the quick.

"There was not a word of truth in the story. An accusation was made, but there was no bottom to it, and it ruffled me. I did not care how much I might be scandalized by enemies of the Church; I had become accustomed to that. I used to say that my hide had got as tough as a hippopotamus; I did not care what an enemy said about me.

"But when an elder in the Church did that it cut me to the heart, and I felt like retaliating. But I sat down and wrote that little poem, 'School thy feelings, O my brother; Train thy warm, impulsive soul,' and so on. And that was for me.

"I did not intend it for anybody else, but it was giving a little counsel to myself."

President Heber J. Grant related some circumstances re-

---

1. *Hymns,* 1985, no. 336.

garding the hymn at October semi-annual General Conference in 1924. He noted that the hymn had been sung in conference and said that he hoped that President Penrose, who was ill, had a radio in his room so he could have heard it.

President Grant said: " . . . I shall not take time to read, or for us to sing, the entire hymn, but I will ask the choir and congregation to arise and sing the first verse and when you go home be sure to read it all. Be sure and get it into your hearts. Be sure and make it a part of your lives, and this conference will not have been in vain."[2]

In an article in the Improvement Era, *Elder Orson F. Whitney of the Council of the Twelve gives us further insight into this unusual story:*

Except for the infamy of his act, I could almost thank "the accuser of the brethren" for that "quiet slander," which wounded the poet's sensitive soul and gave us as the indirect and unintended result this beautiful hymn, which has cheered and comforted for over sixty years the hearts of tens of thousands. Moreover, I will venture to assert that the would-be destroyer of his brother's fair fame did not profit by what he had done, while the one whom he wronged was benefited by the painful experience. Thenceforth he could sympathize, as never before, with those similarly placed. . . .

He went on loving and serving God, and rose step by step to positions of honor and influence, until, in the evening of a long and useful life, we find him standing on the very summit of success, one of the First Presidency of the Church.

And where are they who tried to pull him down? We don't even know their names.[3]

---

2. "An Interesting Story Behind Mormon Hymn," *Church News,* 20 September 1969, p. 7.

3. Orson F. Whitney, "A Hymn With a History," *Improvement Era,* October 1924, pp. 1110, 1112; used by permission.

CHARLES W. PENROSE
O Ye Mountains High

Here is the story of "O Ye Mountains High," in the author's own words. Said President Penrose: " 'Oh Ye Mountains High' was written somewhere along about 1854, published in 1856. I was walking on a dusty road in Essex. My toes were blistered and my heels, too. I had been promised that if I would stay in the mission field another year I should be released. That was the cry every year: 'Brother Penrose, if you will stay and labor another year, we will see that you are released to go to Zion.' But it kept up for over ten years. Of course I had read about Zion and heard about the streets of Salt Lake City, with the clear streams of water on each side of the street, with shade trees, and so on. I could see it in my mind's eye, and so I composed that song as I was walking along the road, and set it to a tune—the Scotch ditty, 'O Minnie, O Minnie, Come o'er the Lea;' those were the opening words. When I got to the place called Mundon, in Essex, we held a cottage meeting, and in that meeting I sang it for the first time it was ever sung. Of course the words were adapted to a person who had never been to Zion then, but it was afterwards changed in a very slight respect or two, to fit people who had gathered with the Saints. It was inspirational and seemed to please President Brigham Young."

When Johnston's army was in Echo Canyon, on its way to Salt Lake City, a Peace Commission, consisting of Governor L. W. Powell of Kentucky, and Major Ben McCullough of Texas, was sent to Utah, arriving at Salt Lake City in June, 1858. In one of the tense meetings (June 11th) the Commissioners presented their message. Brigham Young responded and the outlook for peace seemed favorable. Edward W. Tullidge, in his *History of Salt Lake City,* tells what followed:

"A well-known character, O. P. Rockwell, was seen to enter, approach the ex-Governor and whisper to him. He was from the Mormon army. There was at once a sensation, for it was appreciated that he brought some unexpected and important news. Brigham arose, his manner self-possessed but severe:

" 'Governor Powell, are you aware, sir, that those troops are on the move toward the City?'

" 'It cannot be,' exclaimed Powell, surprised, 'for we were promised by the General that they should not move till after this meeting.'

" 'I have received a dispatch that they are on the march for this City. My messenger would not deceive me.'

"It was like a thunderclap to the Peace Commissioners: they could offer no explanation.

" 'Is Brother Dunbar present?' inquired Brigham.

" 'Yes, sir,' responded the one called. What was coming now?

" 'Brother Dunbar, sing "Zion." ' "

"The Scotch songster came forward and sang — 'O Ye Mountains High.' "

· The song deeply impressed the Peace Commissioners and after several stormy sessions a peaceful solution of the war was agreed upon. The army passed through Salt Lake City, rested temporarily on the west banks of the Jordan River, and then established Camp Floyd on the west side of Utah Lake.

George D. Pyper, *Stories of Latter-day Saint Hymns* (Salt Lake City: Deseret News Press, 1939), pp. 14-16, 17.

JOHN TAYLOR
The Brethren Were Melted to Tears

I DESIRE TO RELATE JUST ONE incident showing how song has the power to soothe irritated feelings and bring harmony to the hearts of men who are filled with a contentious spirit.

The incident occurred some years ago, I have been told, and it was a quarrel between two old Nauvoo veterans. These men had been full of integrity and devotion to the work of the Lord. They had been through many of the hardships of Nauvoo, and had suffered the drivings and persecutions of the Saints, as well as the hardships of pioneering, incident to the early settlement of Salt Lake Valley. These men had quarreled over some business affairs, and finally concluded that they would try and get President John Taylor to help them adjust their difficulties.

John Taylor was then the president of the Council of the Twelve Apostles. The veterans pledged their word of honor, that they would faithfully abide by whatever decision Brother Taylor might render. . . .

They called on President Taylor, but did not immediately tell him what their trouble was, but explained that they had seriously quarreled and asked him if he would listen to their story and render his decision.

President Taylor willingly consented. He said, "Brethren, before I hear your case, I would like very much to sing one of the songs of Zion for you."

Those of my readers who were acquainted with President Taylor know that he was a very capable singer, and interpreted sweetly and with spirit, our sacred hymns. He then sang one of these to the two brethren. Seeing its effect, he remarked that he never heard one of the songs of Zion but that he wanted to listen to one more, and so asked that he might sing another. Of course, they consented. They both seemed to enjoy it; and, having sung the second song, he remarked that with their consent he would sing still another, which he did, as he had heard there is luck in odd numbers. Then in his jocular way, he remarked: "Now brethren, I do not want to wear you out, but if you will forgive me, and listen to one more hymn, I promise to stop singing, and will hear your case."

The story goes that when President Taylor had finished the fourth song, the brethren were melted to tears, got up and shook hands, asked President Taylor to excuse them for having called upon him, and for taking up his time, they then departed without his even knowing what their difficulties were.

President Taylor's singing from our standard hymn book, had reconciled the brethren. The Spirit of the Lord had entered their hearts, and the hills of difference that existed between them, and evidently appeared as big as mountains, had been leveled and become as nothing. Love and brotherhood had developed in their souls, and the trifles over which they had quarreled, had become valueless in their sight. The songs of the heart had filled them with the spirit of reconciliation.

Heber J. Grant, "The Power of Song," *Improvement Era,* May 1919, pp. 634-36; used by permission.

HEBER J. GRANT
It Was a Little Bit Remarkable

I WAS AT A SOCIAL GATHERING IN the home of the late President George Q. Cannon, at that time the first counselor to the president of our church. They had a very splendid dinner, a splendid musical program consisting of instrumental and vocal pieces. Somebody said, "The next number on our program is a song from Brother Grant." This was said as a joke, and everybody laughed. I immediately jumped up and said, "Which of my two songs will you have, 'God Moves in a Mysterious Way, His Wonders to Perform' or 'O My Father, Thou That Dwellest'?"

We were in double parlors. Everybody where I was located said, "God Moves in a Mysterious Way." The accompanist of the evening was in the other room. I asked her to kindly come into the room where the piano was and play that hymn for me in the key of F. Now, I did not know the key of F from any other key, but I had been told that I sung both of the hymns that I had learned in the key of F. When Sister Snow came into the room where I was I whispered to her as she sat down at the piano, that when she got through playing the first verse of the hymn, (I did not mention the name of the hymn to her, taking it for granted that she had heard the request for the hymn "God Moves in a Mysterious Way") I would not know when she was through, but I said, "When you get through with the first verse of this hymn, you just hit this note on the piano, (I tapped the letter F on the piano) and I will commence singing." She did so, and I commenced singing, and my friends at the social gathering commenced laughing and screeching. I paid no attention to them but sang all six verses of "God Moves in a Mysterious Way His Wonders to Perform."

As soon as I finished, I remarked that the ladies and gentlemen present needed lessons in manners, that they had asked me to sing a song, that I had done so and had not made a single solitary mistake, referring to Sister Snow to corroborate my statement, which she did, remarking that "as soon as I started to sing you people commenced laughing and screeching, and I would like to know what you were screeching and laughing at, seeing I made no mistake in singing that song." They assured me that they could not help doing so, and asked if I knew what Sister Snow had done before I started to sing. I told them that I did, announcing that she had played the first verse of "God Moves in a Mysterious Way His Wonders to Perform." They said, "O no, she didn't, she played the first verse of "O My Father, Thou That Dwellest."

I do not wish you to think . . . that I could sing "God Moves in a Mysterious Way" and have someone accompanying me playing "O My Father" — it so happens that the first three words of "O My Father" and the first five words of "God Moves in a Mysterious Way" are on the same note and Mrs. Snow changed immediately when I started to singing a different song, so that she was really accompanying me with the proper melody as soon as I got three words out of my mouth. Inasmuch as I must have practised both of these hymns fully five thousand times before I learned to sing them, it was a little bit remarkable that I did not recognize "O My Father" when she was playing it for me.

"How I Learned to Sing," *In the Native American*, Biographical Pamphlets, Archives of The Church of Jesus Christ of Latter-day Saints, pp. 4-5.

AMANDA SMITH

I'll Never, No Never, No Never Forsake

The following incident was related by Amanda Smith, whose husband and son were killed, and another son seriously wounded at the Haun's Mill Massacre.

ALL THE MORMONS IN THE NEIGHBORHOOD HAD fled out of the State, excepting a few families of the bereaved women and children who had gathered at the house of Brother David Evans, two miles from the scene of the massacre. To this house Alma had been carried after that fatal night.

In our utter desolation, what could we women do but pray. Prayer was our only source of comfort; our Heavenly Father our only Helper. None but he could save and deliver us.

One day a mobber came from the mill with the captain's fiat:

"The captain says if you women don't stop your d—d praying he will send a posse and kill every d—d one of you!"

And he might as well have done it, as to stop us poor women praying in that hour of our great calamity.

Our prayers were hushed in terror. We dared not let our voices be heard in the house in supplication. I could pray in my bed or in silence, but I could not live thus long. This godless silence was more intolerable than had been that night of the massacre.

I could bear it no longer. I pined to hear once more my own voice in petition to my Heavenly Father.

I stole down into a corn-field, and crawled into a "stout of corn." It was as the temple of the Lord to me at that moment. I prayed aloud and most fervently.

When I emerged from the corn, a voice spoke to me. It was a voice as plain as I ever heard one. It was no silent, strong impression of the spirit, but a *voice,* repeating a verse of the saint's hymn:

> The soul that on Jesus hath leaned for repose
> I will not, I cannot, desert to his foes;
> That soul, though all hell should endeavor to shake,
> I'll never, no never, no never forsake![1]

From that moment I had no more fear. I felt that nothing could hurt me. Soon after this the mob sent us word that unless we were all out of the State by a certain day we should be killed.

The day came, and at evening came fifty armed men to execute the sentence.

I met them at the door. They demanded of me why I was not gone? I bade them enter and see their own work. They crowded into my room and I showed them my wounded boy. They came, party after party, until all had seen my excuse. Then they quarreled among themselves and came near fighting.

At last they went away, all but two. These I thought were detailed to kill us. Then the two returned.

"Madam," said one, "have you any meat in the house?"

"No," was my reply.

"Could you dress a fat hog if one were laid at your door?"

"I think we could!" was my answer.

And then they went and caught a fat hog from a herd which had belonged to a now exiled brother, killed it and dragged it to my door, and departed.

These men, who had come to murder us, left on the threshold of our door a meat offering to atone for their repented intention. . . .

The Lord had kept His word. The soul that on Jesus had leaned for succcor had not been forsaken even in this terrible hour of massacre.

---

1. *Hymns,* 1985, no. 85.

Edward W. Tullidge, *The Women of Mormondom* (New York: Tullidge & Crandall, 1877), pp. 129-32.

VESSA MCGRATH
When through the Deep Waters

VESSA MCGRATH, A GRANDMOTHER IN Duncan, Arizona, found spiritual comfort in the hymns. Her husband, Vernon, had been home from the hospital only a few days when a flood washed through the town. Then six weeks later, Vernon died.

"My problems compounded," says Vessa. "I was in a dark cloud so far as knowing what to do about the business and many other things. Every day I prayed earnestly to find a solution. One night, while I was lying awake trying to make some decisions, it suddenly seemed like I was looking at a screen with words on it:

> When through the deep waters I call thee to go,
> The rivers of sorrow shall not thee o'erflow,
> For I will be with thee, thy troubles to bless,
> And sanctify to thee thy deepest distress.[1]

"No words have had greater impact upon my mind. The next morning I found them in the hymnbook — 'How Firm a Foundation.' As I read the rest of the hymn, it seemed that every word was written especially for me.

"My personal relationship with the Lord became more important to me," Sister McGrath says. "Without his help I could not have made it, even with all the kindness from people and the concern of my family."

---

1. *Hymns,* 1985, no. 85.

Marvin K. Gardner, "When Disaster Strikes," *Ensign,* January 1982, pp. 70-71; used by permission.

WM. JAMES MORTIMER
It Still Gives Me Strength

I WAS JUST TWENTY-NINE WHEN I was called to be a bishop. The call came on Wednesday evening and I was to be sustained the following Sunday. Throughout those few days before I was to be sustained, through worry and anxiety, I was wondering how it would all work out. Earnestly and humbly I prayed for strength. While I was praying, there came to me with great comfort and a feeling of strength, the third verse of the hymn, "How Firm a Foundation":

> Fear not, I am with thee; oh be not dismayed,
> For I am thy God and will still give thee aid.
> I'll strengthen thee, help thee, and cause thee to stand,
> Upheld by my righteous, omnipotent hand.[1]

It was an answer to my prayer, a direct answer by inspiration to my fearful prayers and it gave me strength. From that point on I never worried but proceeded to do what I was called to do.

Since then, every time I sing that hymn I have the same feeling come back to me reminding me of the direct answer to my prayer. Oftentimes, now as I experience feelings of despair, I remember that experience and my strength is renewed all over again.

---

1. *Hymns,* 1985, no. 85.

Unpublished; used by permission.

W. HERBERT KLOPFER
My Heart Was Touched

IN MAY 1957, ONE HUNDRED SAINTS from the German Democratic Republic spent one week in the Swiss Temple receiving their temple ordinances. They came to the temple in two specially chartered trains. They brought with them the lame, the blind, and other handicapped Saints. They had sacrificed all of their savings to make the trip. I served as a young missionary at the Swiss Temple and was overwhelmed by the demonstration of their strong faith. I felt the greatest love for them as I took charge, welcomed them, and gave them instructions regarding money, food, and accommodations.

We served them breakfast every morning. But we had to trim back to the simple foods of bread and milk since their bodies were not able to assimilate more nutritious foods. Lunches were served free of charge. I assisted them in practically every phase of temple work as they literally worked around the clock receiving their own ordinances and performing the same for as many of their deceased ancestors as time permitted. I averaged four hours of sleep each night because of the need for constant service.

My three living grandparents were part of this group. I did not know that they were coming until I saw their names on the official list. It was a joyous and memorable reunion (the last in their mortal lifetime) as I helped them receive their temple ordinances by serving simultaneously as temple worker and family proxy. I witnessed their own endowments and subsequent sealings to their deceased relatives, including my own father.

When the time of departure came, these Saints sang "How Firm a Foundation" with all their hearts as they assembled in the cultural hall of the nearby chapel for final instructions. Then, at the train station, they bid farewell by singing, "God Be With You 'Til We Meet Again." The spiritual power generated by these two hymns was enough to lift these wonderful Saints for the remainder of their mortal days. They knew that, most likely, they would not enter a temple of the Lord again while in this probationary state of life. But they had made covenants with the Lord in the Swiss Temple and now relied on the power of hymns to sustain them in their desire to live acceptable lives before their God even though deprived of many basic freedoms.

Unpublished; used by permission.

W. HERBERT KLOPFER

Fellowship with the Saints through the Tune of a Hymn

IN THE YEARS OF WORLD WAR II, my father served simultaneously as president of the East German Mission and a mandatory tour of duty in the German army. He directed the affairs of the mission from the battlefield through his capable counselors. Our family saw him for the last time in November 1943 while he was on furlough. The mission home in Berlin had been completely destroyed at that time, and our family was evacuated to central Germany. My father was sent to Denmark. What happened to him there and subsequent other locations is a matter of record in personal journals of others since we did not see our father again before his starvation death in March 1945 in Russia.

My father was stationed in or near Esbjerg in Denmark in December 1943. He was very lonely and wanted to go to sacrament meeting on one of the two Sundays preceding Christmas. He did not know whether or not there was a branch of the Church in Esbjerg but he assumed that there was one somewhere in the city. He was in enemy country dressed in full military uniform and did not speak the language. He recognized that music would be understood anywhere, so he hummed the tune of a favorite hymn as he walked on a city street in hopes of attracting someone's attention who would recognize the tune and would lead him to the place of worship.

A little girl skipped along the sidewalk on her way to Church. As she passed my father, she recognized the tune and asked him in Danish: "Mormon?" He nodded his head. She took him by the hand and led him to the branch meetingplace.

His arrival at the backdoor created a tense moment for the assembled Saints. Who was this man in enemy uniform? Was he there to do harm? The branch president was concerned as he stood at the pulpit ready to begin sacrament meeting. He stopped and walked to the backdoor to find out who my father was. After my father had identified himself and added that he was anxious to worship the Lord with the Saints, the branch president invited him to come with him to the podium and deliver the gospel message this day. He did so in beautiful English, since German was not very appreciated by the Danes.

My father chanced his life going to sacrament meeting in an enemy country, realizing that his likely discovery by Nazi officials among enemy people in their worship services would bring upon him a charge of treason or the like, punishable by death. This chance was further amplified by his surrendering his weapon belt to the branch president at the backdoor and taking an active part in the meeting. But his desire to worship the Lord was stronger than the cords of death. And he had been led to the place of worship by the power of the Lord. A little girl provided my father fellowship with the Saints because of the simple power of a familiar hymn tune.

Unpublished; used by permission.

NEAL A. MAXWELL
I Remember What We Sang

It's just about forty springs ago that a battered group of infantrymen assembled on a little hill on Okinawa, our division having been relieved, I attended an LDS service, the first we'd had since the fighting had begun. We were anxious to be there and see who had survived and who would not show. As we began that meeting singing "Come, Come, Ye Saints," we watched carefully to see who might yet come, even though we knew when certain individuals didn't come, they'd been killed or had been wounded.

I don't remember a thing that was said at that meeting but I remember what we sang. Often in life this is true of us.

I'm so grateful that "I Am a Child of God" is in the hymnbook along with the great traditional anthems that are here. When we're separated from each other and on special occasions, the music and lyrics can course through our minds in a way that will permit us to be steadfast, to be grateful, and to be reassured. In that sense, this [new hymnbook] is not alone a gathering of hymns for us to sing in our meetings, which is reason enough, but it is the means by which the rising generation can learn the hymns of Zion and carry them in their minds and in their hearts withersoever they will go.

Unpublished address delivered at the 1985 Hymnbook Celebration in the Temple Square Assembly Hall, Salt Lake City, 3 September 1985; used by permission.

JAY CRIDDLE HESS

The Hymns Provided Me with the Greatest Lessons

Major Hess was a United States Air Force pilot. Shot down on August 24, 1967, he spent five and one-half years in prisoner of war camps near Hanoi and close to the Chinese border.

As a prisoner of war I was stripped of every material thing that I owned. I was isolated from any contact with the outside world. It was a bad situation to be in, but it provided me with a period of reflection and meditation such as I had never had before. . . .

Some of my fellow prisoners felt alone, and they were in need of help. I felt that I had complete support from whatever source I needed. I enjoyed a closeness to God. There was no fear; it was almost a time of warmth. I suppose I really can't say there was no fear, because I well remember the nights when the guards would come and open the doors of cells around me. There was always fear that they might be coming to my door. Every night I could hear them coming to take people out for questioning or for moving to other cells. Chains rattled, people would be moaning; it was kind of a horror show.

The hymns of the Church provided me with the greatest lessons during this time. I couldn't remember all of them, of course, and even now I can't remember more than one verse of any song. But the phrases from one hymn, one verse from another, and parts of others gave me gospel lessons when I needed them.

One such phrase was "Come, come, ye Saints, no toil nor labor fear." I would think of that song on days that were tough and say to myself, "That is a great lesson for me right there. Don't fear, just do whatever you have to do." And the last verse: "And should we die before our journey's through, happy day!"

There were a lot of days just like that. It would have been happiness to have died that day, but I knew that if I could make it through, then I was going to be really happy. So it gave a balance to my life in prison.

I remember once when I got hold of some paper and made a pen; using blue iodine for ink, I wrote down as many hymns as I could remember. I listed about a hundred. Hymns were used in my prayers, like the one the children sing in Primary: "Lead me, guide me, walk beside me...." However, I didn't apply the words to myself, but turned them around. Don't teach *me* or guide *me;* rather, lead my children and guide them.

The first chance I got to write home, the main thing I had on my mind was to assure my family that the things that are valuable and important are those that have to do with the Church. I tried to put emphasis on family home evening, proper education, missions, temple marriage, and a family history.

"Eternal Values Sustained Prisoner of War," *Ensign,* June 1973, pp. 70, 71; used by permission.

GILBERT SCHARFFS
The Elder Started to Whistle

IN JULY 1939 MORMON APOSTLE Joseph Fielding Smith toured parts of Germany. . . . As the crisis [which was to become World War II] intensified, Apostle Smith waited in anticipation. On August 24, 1939, a week before the invasion of Poland, the First Presidency of the Church ordered the . . . evacuation [of the missionaries from Germany]. . . .

President Wood of the West German Mission and President Joseph Fielding Smith were in Hanover holding a missionary conference when the evacuation orders arrived. An hour and twenty minutes later the mission president was at mission headquarters in Frankfurt to direct the missionary evacuation. The plane taken by the Woods was the last civilian flight made by this aircraft before being sent to the Polish front.

There were about 150 American missionaries in the two German missions and telegrams were sent to each pair to rush to Holland. The Dutch consul in Frankfurt agreed to allow the missionaries to enter the Netherlands. . . .

Early Saturday morning, the 26th, one of the elders . . . called by phone from the Netherlands border. He said, "President Wood, we have been here for six hours and the Dutch will not let us in. We haven't a dime between us. What shall we do?" The Dutch had recollections of the previous war and didn't want anyone entering their country who would have to be fed. . . .

About the same time, a radio announcement was made by the government stating that "after Sunday night at midnight, August 27, the German government would not guarantee anyone his destination on German railways." The German Army was being mobilized. "I shall never forget our feelings at this time," said the mission president, and continued, "we had no telegraph, nor telephone facilities and railways were not available to us. We were not able to contact our missionaries, and

61

we knew that most of them would be heading toward the closed Netherlands border. . . .

"We knew they would arrive there without enough money to buy tickets for Denmark," said Wood. Time was against the missionaries, because all of the railroads would be used for troop transportation within forty-eight hours. Later the president related the way some of the missionaries were rescued:

"About this time a big former football player came into our office who weighed over 200 pounds. I said, 'Brother, did you ever carry a message to Garcia?'

"He said, 'No, I haven't, but I'm willing to try.'

"I said: 'Elder, we have thirty-one missionaries lost somewhere between here and the Dutch border. It will be your mission to find them and see that they get out.' "

This elder set out for his destination with five hundred marks and tickets for Denmark and London. The president had heard that a person could get into Holland if he had tickets for Great Britain. Wood continued his account of the experience of this elder: "After four hours on the train he arrived at Cologne, which is about half way to the Dutch border. We had told him to follow his impressions entirely as we had no idea what towns these elders would be in. Cologne was not his destination, but he felt inspired to get off the train there. It is a very large station and was then filled with thousands of people. There were many students returning to England, and many people returning from vacation before the train service was to be stopped. There were so many people that to find anyone would have been next to impossible. This elder started to whistle our missionary song—'Do What Is Right, Let the Consequence Follow.'

"Down in one corner of the station was an elder, with an old couple who were also on a mission from America. They were stranded at the Cologne station and couldn't call the mission office because no more calls were being accepted. These three were able to pass through Holland with their tickets."

The elder continued toward the border and stopped in those towns where he "felt the urge and gave the 'Mormon whistle call'." He found several more missionaries in that manner. . . .

Meanwhile, President Joseph Fielding Smith and his wife had left Hanover for Frankfurt by train. When they arrived, President Wood had left them a message and tickets for London via Holland. President Smith was one of the last to enter that country.

Mormonism in Germany (Salt Lake City: Deseret Book, 1970), pp. 92-95.

THREE

TEACHING ONE ANOTHER WITH HYMNS

Let the word of Christ dwell in you richly in all wisdom; teaching and admonishing one another in psalms and hymns and spiritual songs, singing with grace in your hearts to the Lord. (Colossians 3:16.)

EZRA TAFT BENSON
When I Was Called as a Scoutmaster

I SHALL ALWAYS BE GRATEFUL THAT ALMOST sixty-five years ago the good bishop of our ward came to me and asked me to be Scoutmaster of twenty-four boys in the Whitney Ward. . . . This was a great group of young men with a lot of musical talent.

In those days we had in the Mutual various cultural activities which were competitive. Among them were boys' choruses. Each ward was expected to have a chorus, and ofttimes the bishop would invite the Scoutmaster to take the responsibility for getting the boys out to practice. So it was in our ward.

As is often the case when a man is asked to do a job, I sought out the help of a good faithful woman who could play the piano and knew some musical technique. Under her direction we started our practices. The song to be sung in the competition was assigned by the general board and was the same throughout the Church — "The Morning Breaks; the Shadows Flee," by Parley P. Pratt.

For weeks before and after Scout meetings we prepared. Finally the time came when we would meet in competition with the ten other wards of the Franklin Stake. We were successful in winning in the stake, and then we were to meet the winners of the six other stakes in Cache Valley in the tabernacle in Logan.

I shall never forget approaching that great tabernacle that evening. We went inside and drew for places. We drew last place, which only prolonged our anxiety.

Finally the time came that our group was to march up to the platform. As our accompanist played "The Stars and Stripes Forever," those twenty-four boys went up the aisle single file and formed in a half moon on the stage while I crouched down between a couple of benches to try to give them some leadership. Then they sang as I'd never heard them sing, and of course you can imagine that I'd not be telling this story had we not won first place in Logan.

We went home literally walking on air. We were so happy that this little community of fifty families had won over the other stakes and wards of the valley.

In the first Scout meeting following our victory, those boys (never forgetting anything that is of value to them) reminded me that in a moment of anxiety I had promised them that if we won in Logan, I would take them all on a hike over the mountain thirty-five miles to Bear Lake Valley.

Since a promise made is a debt unpaid, we began planning our hike. . . . [Soon] we left on that great thirty-five-mile Scout trip to which I had made commitment as an inducement to get the boys out to practice their singing. . . . It was a glorious three weeks together with those wonderful boys out in the hills and in the mountains and on the lake. I wish I could follow for you the life of each one of those boys from that time until the present. I am proud of them.

I have made an effort to keep in touch with these boys. . . . So far as we know, [all] of the twenty-four [were] married in the temple. Some of them have gone now, but we have good reason to suppose each one did a good job in life.

In Conference Report, October 1984, pp. 60-61; used by permission.

GORDON B. HINCKLEY

A Great and Marvelous Statement

THE WORDS [OF THE HYMN "The Spirit of God Like a Fire Is Burning"] were written by W. W. Phelps. What a great and marvelous statement that is, sung for the first time, [according to] the record of our history, at the dedication of the Kirtland Temple in 1836. . . .

It has been my opportunity in the last twenty-eight months to participate in the dedication of seventeen new temples. In those dedicatory services the choirs have sung, "The Morning Breaks, the Shadows Flee." And the concluding number sung by the choir in each dedicatory service is the "Hosanna Anthem," which was written by Evan Stephens, the shepherd boy from the Welsh hills who joined the Church and came to Zion and composed much of our greatest music — distinctive, beautiful, Latter-day Saint music. The choir has sung the "Hosanna Anthem" and the congregation, in each of these dedicatory services, has then joined in singing, "The Spirit of God Like a Fire Is Burning." In each of these situations I have sat with the choir immediately behind me, and the members of the choir have always had difficulty singing because of the tears that choke their voices as they try to express themselves in a newly dedicated House of God.

In these dedicatory services we have joined through the music three great events in the history of the Church: the dedication of the first temple in 1836; the dedication of the Salt Lake Temple in 1893; and the dedication of the new temple.

Unpublished talk delivered at the 1985 Hymnbook Celebration in the Temple Square Assembly Hall, Salt Lake City, 3 September 1985; used by permission.

EUGENE ENGLAND

Welded Together in Spiritual Unity and Power and Beauty

Rᴇᴄᴇɴᴛʟʏ I ᴘᴀʀᴛɪᴄɪᴘᴀᴛᴇᴅ ɪɴ . . . ᴀ Mᴏʀᴍᴏɴ artistic endeavor—one of the dedication sessions in the Solemn Assembly Room of the Washington Temple. At the climax of the service, after we had all stood to express our joy in that unique Mormon ritual of celebration, the "Hosanna Shout" following the dedicatory prayer, a volunteer choir, which like nine others for the other sessions had traveled by bus hundreds of miles from one of the various regions in the Temple District, remained standing in their places to the side of the room, facing at an angle both the audience on the main floor and the General Authorities and other leaders on the stand, and sang the "Hosanna Anthem." We, our leaders, and the choir, all still standing and facing each other, then joined in singing at the anthem's close, "The Spirit of God Like a Fire Is Burning" while the choir voices soared above us in a descant, welding us together in one unbroken ring of—not aesthetically great art, perhaps, but what is much more important, unparalleled spiritual unity and power and beauty which the musical quality of the choir (diminished partly by the emotion they felt along with all of us) did not create but did in fact contribute to. I've heard and deeply appreciate some great music, written and performed by great musicians, including some great religious music by people of sincere faith, but I have never experienced any other music nearly as moving—or pleasing—or "worthwhile" as that singing in the Temple.

Eugene England, "Book Review of *A Believing People: Literature of the Latter-day Saints,* Richard H. Cracroft and Neal E. Lambert, eds.," in *Brigham Young University Studies,* Spring 1975 (Provo, Utah: Brigham Young University Press, 1975), pp. 365-66.

SPENCER W. KIMBALL
I Need Thee Every Hour

I THINK THE LORD IS HAPPY when He hears us say, "I *need* thee." And when he feels that we really do need Him. I would like us to sing it — "I *need* thee — OH, I need thee!" I always tell the missionaries to sing it that way — to give that emphasis on, "I need thee! How much I need thee! How limited I am, how alone I am if You are not with me." So we sing, "I need thee every hour, most gracious Lord."

And then at night, before we retire, we get our families together, and we say, "I need thee *every* hour." Then when we get up in the mornings, before we go to school and seminary and elsewhere, we say to the Lord, one of us of the family, "I need thee, oh, I need thee. Today in my lessons, in my associations, in my friendships — I need Thee, *every* hour, most gracious Lord." I hope you sing it with that intent.

Unpublished address delivered at dedication of the Mormon Center Complex, Fair Oaks, California Stake, Fair Oaks, California, 9 October 1976.

SPENCER W. KIMBALL

President Kimball Himself Played "I Need Thee Every Hour"

UPON THE SUDDEN AND UNEXPECTED DEATH OF his beloved friend Harold B. Lee, the mantle of the prophet rested upon Spencer Kimball. He said, "We prayed it would never happen; our prayers were for President Harold B. Lee. Night and morning every day we prayed for a long life and the general welfare of President Lee. I knew the responsibility could fall to me, but I did not seek it. Now I will do my best." (*Church News,* 5 January 1974, p. 4.)

On December 30, 1973, the brethren gathered in the Salt Lake Temple to sustain and set apart the new President of the Church. As they convened, President Kimball himself played "I Need Thee Every Hour" on the piano and the apostles sang. Then each of them in turn bore his witness that Spencer Kimball was the man the Lord wanted to preside over the Church.

Lawrence R. Flake, *Mighty Men of Zion* (Salt Lake City: Deseret Press, 1974), p. 69; used by permission.

BOYD K. PACKER
The Inspiration of Sacred Music

THIS IS WHAT I WOULD TEACH YOU. Choose from among the sacred music of the Church a favorite hymn, one with words that are uplifting and music that is reverent, one that makes you feel something akin to inspiration. . . . Go over it in your mind carefully. Memorize it. Even though you have had no musical training, you can think through a hymn.

Now, use this hymn as the place for your thoughts to go. Make it your emergency channel. Whenever you find these shady actors have slipped from the sidelines of your thinking onto the stage of your mind, put on this record, as it were.

As the music begins and as the words form in your thoughts, the unworthy ones will slip shamefully away. It will change the whole mood on the stage of your mind. Because it is uplifting and clean, the baser thoughts will disappear. For while virtue, by choice, *will not* associate with filth, evil *cannot* tolerate the presence of light.

In due time you will find yourself, on occasion, humming the music inwardly. As you retrace your thoughts, you discover some influence from the world about you encouraged an unworthy thought to move on stage in your mind, and the music almost automatically began.

"Music," said Gladstone, "Is one of the most forceful instruments for governing the mind and spirit of man."

I am so grateful for music that is worthy and uplifting and inspiring.

In Conference Report, October 1973, pp. 24-25; used by permission.

ARDETH GREENE KAPP
How Gentle God's Commands

SEVERAL WEEKS AGO . . . I was asked to participate in an institute program and speak to a gathering of men in a small chapel. These men had an understanding of law, agency, freedom, blessings, choice, and accountability. To reach the chapel I had to go through tight security, present identification, be escorted by an officer of the law down a long corridor through sets of metal doors with bars which sounded a haunting echo as the metal clanged against metal. As each door in sequence closed tightly behind me, I knew I was locked in. There was no doubt in my mind about that. As I, with a friend, proceeded down the long corridor, there were odors revealing habits of enslavement. As we approached the chapel we heard a sound which seemed foreign to that setting—beautiful male voices harmonizing with feeling. Entering the meeting that was already in session, I observed each man wearing the same uniform. It wasn't a dark suit and white shirt, although I learned that more than one of them had worn a missionary suit. Their uniforms each had an identification number across the area of their hearts.

Looking at their numbers I wondered, "Who are they really?" Almost everyone was holding one of the new green hymnbooks. Would you be interested in knowing what song these men who had made choices that robbed them of their freedom and put them behind bars were singing? I wish you could hear that song sung by these men—"How Gentle God's Commands." I'll never hear that song again without reliving that experience. Listen with me to the words:

> How gentle God's commands!
> How kind his precepts are!
> Come, cast your burdens on the Lord
> And trust his constant care.
> Beneath his watchful eye,

His saints securely dwell;
That hand which bears all nature up
Shall guard his children well.
Why should this anxious load
Press down your weary mind?
Haste to your Heav'nly Father's throne
And sweet refreshment find.
His goodness stands approved,
Unchanged from day to day;
I'll drop my burden at his feet
And bear a song away.[1]

---

1. *Hymns,* 1985, no. 125.

"Your Inheritance: Secure or in Jeopardy?" in *Brigham Young University 1986-87 Devotional and Fireside Speeches* (Provo: University Publications, 1987), pp. 99-100; used by permission.

JOSEPH WALKER
The Hymns Are My Sermons

THE DEAF WOMAN HAD BEEN COMING TO church faithfully for years, rarely missing a service. She seldom was able to sit close enough to the front to be able to read the lips of the speakers, but still she came and seemed to bask in the spirit of each meeting. One day she was asked why she kept coming when she could never receive the message of the speakers.

"I can read the words of the hymns as you sing them," she said tenderly. "The hymns are my sermons."

"Hymns—Sermons in Four-Four Time," *Church News,* 28 March 1981, p. 5.

PAUL N. DAVIS

Preparing Myself Spiritually to Give a Patriarchal Blessing

UNTIL RECENTLY, MY CHURCH EXPERIENCE had been primarily administrative — as a bishop, stake high councilor, stake executive secretary, counselor in the stake presidency, and stake president for almost ten years. However, a few years after my release as stake president I was called to be a patriarch. As a stake president I had worked closely with patriarchs and had great admiration for them but had often thought, "There's something special about those men and I know that I could never be that." So I accepted this call with some trepidation.

In all new callings I had experienced the normal quandaries of where do you go and what do you do, how do you get inspiration, and how do you know when you're guided? My personal credo has been, "Work hard to get the facts and then try to make an inspired decision in relation to everything you can possibly know." And, over twenty years, I had had the benefit of counselors to counsel with. As problems arose, of course we had prayer, but I also always enjoyed the counsel of wise men.

But this was a whole different ballgame. There was no one to counsel with. It wasn't even like setting apart missionaries, where you are dealing with people you know well and for a period of only eighteen months or two years. Now you're talking with someone regarding their eternal life, and without that basis of working knowledge. And, especially, there's no one to counsel with.

In a training meeting with our area presidency, we were told that we should "just be guided by the Spirit." I tried to get ready. I would begin by cleansing myself physically with a shower and fresh clothing. Beyond that, I was concerned and wondered, "Now, how do I do it? How do I get prepared? How do I leave the world?"

I remembered taking one of my children for a patriarchal blessing and the patriarch had some classical music playing. So I went and bought some Tabernacle Choir religious tapes and others that had Mormon hymns. Now I go into a separate room and turn on those tapes. I have them all categorized and I hope that I'm prompted in the ones that I pick out. I start listening to them and pretty soon I find myself singing along with them and sometimes even in harmony with them. There are thoughts that then start coming to me—I figure you can't draw water from an empty well and I'm hoping that those thoughts will come into my mind as I am doing the work of a patriarch. I had the mistaken impression that I would close my eyes and see and then I would just have to dictate what I would see. And others may do that but it's not my experience. And so, I generally listen to sacred music for an hour and then I read the scriptures. For me, it's a combination of sacred music and scripture reading. Sometimes I will get out the hymnbook and just read the words but usually I like to hear them sung. I want to hear the hymns that I'm familiar with, hymns that have a message to them.

There are other beautiful hymns—one of my favorites is, "Fair are the meadows, fair are the woodlands." I love that one and it's inspirational to me as far as the mood is concerned. But as for my thoughts, it does not speak to my mind in this experience. I listened to them sing "O Divine Redeemer" in one of the devotionals in the temple one time and I loved it and it was powerful and moving, but it doesn't do for me what the hymns do. The hymnbook, to me, is a sacred scriptural text, just like the Book of Mormon, the Doctrine and Covenants, and so on. And the hymns contained in it are the ones which seem to fulfill my need to prepare my mind for my patriarchal calling. Strangely enough, in my experience, the hymns— whether sung by the choir, a soloist, by myself, or just con- templated—serve the valuable function of removing my thoughts from the cares of the world and putting me in tune with the Spirit. I don't mean to say that this is the only way it can be done, but it is the only way I know of that works for me.

Unpublished; used by permission.

ROBERT L. SIMPSON
We Sang Hymns on Red Square

Elder Simpson tells the following story that happened on a trip he and Sister Simpson took into Eastern Europe with the Brigham Young University International Folk Dancers:

AT RED SQUARE WE MET A WONDERFUL MAN who also loves the Church but has never been baptized. He wanted to meet us on Red Square just before we left on the last day. And there, out of his little briefcase he took a copy of the three-in-one, and turning to the Doctrine and Covenants read at the top of his voice on Red Square what the Lord said to his children about being patient and waiting on the Lord's kindness, and eventually all would come. There were guards around, and we were a little nervous. But then he made one last request: would we please sing "Come, Come, Ye Saints" for him? So we sang "Come, Come, Ye Saints" at the tops of our voices, and we felt so good about that that we also sang "God Be With You Till We Meet Again." Then this man put his scriptures back into his bag and said good-bye. Hopefully there will be a time when he will be able to receive the fulness of the gospel.

"Unto All People," in *Devotional Speeches of the Year, 1979* (Provo: Brigham Young University Press, 1980), p. 177; used by permission.

HUGH W. PINNOCK
The Singing of Hymns Had Saved the Day

M USIC HAS THE ABILITY TO SOOTHE AND COMFORT, to positively change our moods and the way we feel. Lively music can give us a lift when we are feeling down. Spiritual music facilitates our feeling the Spirit and worshipping sensitively. Music plays an important role in the Church because of its power to affect each of us. . . . Hymns have [always] been the core of music in the Church. Hymns are an especially powerful tool because the music brings back pleasant feelings of past experiences, and the words convey gospel messages that can be memorized and recorded.

I remember attending a stake conference in Victoria, Mexico. We were struggling to have the conference be a meaningful, spiritual experience for those attending.

Two well-organized choirs were seated on separate sides of the chapel. They began our Sunday morning session with some of the most beautiful music to which I have ever listened. Suddenly, we all knew the conference was going to be a success. And it was. As it ended, we left motivated to live a more gospel-oriented life. Part of our desires were due, in part, to the beautiful music that had motivated each of the speakers and communicated to us the spirit of our Heavenly Father.

Another sweet experience involving the hymns occurred when I was meeting with a group of single adults on a misty morning in Cape Cod, Massachusetts. The weather had turned unseasonably cold. It was apparent that there were negative emotions among so many who were present that morning. One of the lovely single sisters from Boston suggested we sing a few hymns before our morning fireside began. Soon, everyone was smiling. The singing of hymns had saved the day.

"Collection of Hymns, Old and New, Will Serve Varied Needs of Members," *Church News,* 11 August 1985, p. 4.

ROBERT L. SIMPSON
Effect of Church Hymns

Let me tell you briefly about a man who was attending a patio party one Sunday afternoon at the home of a business associate who happened to live next door to an LDS meetinghouse. As the sacrament meeting got underway, the strains of the organ could be clearly heard over the back fence and seemed to be somewhat incongruous to the tinkle of ice being placed in the cocktail glasses. There were some uncomplimentary jokes and the usual snide remarks about religious fanatics, when all of a sudden the strains of the opening song broke the warm summer afternoon air. It was "Come, Come, Ye Saints." The party tempo was warming up, and by now, the church music was all but unnoticed — unnoticed by all but one, a man whose grandmother had walked across the plains pulling a handcart. His mind withdrew from the party. For the first time in many years, he spent some minutes in sincere reflection concerning his birthright.

About ten minutes later, the sacrament song came drifting across the back fence. Unknowingly, a chorister, inspired in her calling, I am sure, had selected, "I Know That My Redeemer Lives." And way down deep, he knew it, too, but it had been a long, long time. From that moment on, he was attending a patio party in body, but mentally and spiritually he was far above and beyond his environment of the moment.

It was almost an hour later, just about the time that he had lapsed back into the party mood, when the closing song, "We Thank Thee, O God, For a Prophet," reached his ear and mellowed his heart to the point of submission. Isn't it odd that a man should start his way back while attending a cocktail party? "The Lord moves in a mysterious way, His wonders to perform." Incidentally, that man is probably here in this meeting today, a fine leader in the church, doing what the Lord would have him do.

In Conference Report, October 1969, pp. 10-11; used by permission.

BARBARA K. CHRISTENSEN
Singing with Elder Kimball

IT HAPPENED IN THE DAYS WHEN stake conferences consisted of two sessions during the day and a stake fireside in the evening. The visiting General Authority always attended the 10 A.M. and the 2 P.M. sessions and occasionally remained as the speaker for the evening fireside. On one particular day it was our good fortune in the Wasatch Stake (Heber City, Utah) to have Elder Spencer W. Kimball as the guest for the day. Our family had been somewhat acquainted with Elder Kimball and were overjoyed when he accepted our invitation to have dinner with us and remain at our home until time for the evening session.

My eight sisters and I[1] did a great deal of singing during the time we grew up and were accustomed to invitations that didn't give us a great deal of time for preparation. However, on that conference afternoon, the telephone rang and I heard the voice of our stake president, H. Clay Cummings, on the other end. He told me that the person previously asked to sing the musical number for the evening fireside couldn't perform and wondered if our family would provide some music. I placed my hand over the phone while I relayed the message and asked the others for their opinion. I mentioned to them that it was extremely short notice and that perhaps we should tell him no.

While a short discussion ensued, our guest taught us all a great lesson: "Tell President Cummings *we'd* love to," Elder Kimball remarked. "Your father and I will do the men's parts and two of you girls can do the others and we'll sing them one of the beautiful hymns."

I sheepishly gave the message to President Cummings and hung up the phone. Immediately, we gathered around the piano and prepared our presentation for the evening.

---

1. Barbara K. Christensen is the wife of Joe J. Christensen, President of Ricks College and former Commissioner of the Church Educational System.

Can you imagine the thrill of singing that number with a member of the Quorum of the Twelve and the future president of the Church? It was an experience I shall never forget.

"Singing with Elder Kimball," *Ensign,* March 1982, p. 12; used by permission.

DELILA G. WILLIAMS
We Shared a Song

O<small>N A RECENT TOUR OF</small> B<small>IBLE LANDS</small>, I was struck by one cleaning woman's pleasant appearance and cheerful acceptance of the duties required of her. Toward the end of our stay I happened to be alone with this woman for a few moments. We exchanged greetings, so I knew she spoke English. Impulsively, I asked her to sing me a song of her childhood. Her dark eyes shone, and I knew my request had pleased her. After thinking for a moment, she sang a song in a language I did not understand. When she stopped singing, I said, "Tell me what it means."

She replied, "It is Arabic and a song of Jesus, who loves me. Now, will you sing one to me?"

I sang my favorite, "Jesus Once Was a Little Child," learned in Primary years ago. After the first phrase, I was surprised to hear her join me, and we sang together the rest of the verse. I could hardly believe it. In spite of the differences of our cultures and nearly nine thousand miles between our homes, our hearts were in the same place—filled with joy shared in a child's song of Jesus.

"We Shared a Song," *Ensign*, April 1982, p. 55; used by permission.

WANDA WEST BADGER
Singing Brought Us Together

W HEN OUR STAKE OFFERED TO HOUSE a group of Saints from Mexico who were coming to Salt Lake City to attend the temple for a week, we agreed to have at least two guests in our home. No one in my family knew a word of Spanish, and I was concerned about communicating with them. The day soon came when my husband ushered in two smiling guests, a man and his wife, who greeted me with "Buenos Dias!" They knew no English—not a word. My heart sank. How would I get through the week?

The first evening, a friend who could speak some Spanish interpreted for us. The next evening she wasn't available, and I felt self-conscious as my guests sat and watched me preparing dinner, clearing up, and puttering around at other chores. Unconsciously, and I suppose to help break the silence, I began humming a hymn.

Immediately Brother Regino's eyes lit up. He started singing the same hymn in Spanish and finished the song with me. He started another familiar hymn and I joined him with English. His wife and my family soon joined us, and with delighted smiles we continued singing until we exhausted all the songs we knew. By then we felt the warmth of being close to one another, even without knowing the other's language.

I have always cherished that week the Mexican Saints were with us, because I learned one important thing—that people who share the gospel of Jesus Christ are "of one heart and of one soul" (Acts 4:32), and language is no longer a barrier.

"Singing Brought Us Together," *Ensign*, March 1985, p. 14; used by permission.

FOUR

REMEMBERING THE SONGS OF YOUTH

The Lord says, "the song of the heart" is a prayer to him and that it shall be answered with a blessing upon our heads. I have a song in my home every morning, since I learned to sing, and I feel that it is a nice part of the family worship, and I feel that we can increase the capacity of our children to sing and to praise the Lord in the songs of Zion, if we will only teach them to sing over and over again. (Heber J. Grant, in Conference Report, April 1900, p. 62.)

JOSEPH F. SMITH AND JOSEPH FIELDING SMITH

The Hymns He Sang Became Familiar to Me

Joseph F. Smith and his son Joseph Fielding Smith reminisce about their fathers and hymn singing in their homes, in a strikingly parallel manner.

"I can remember when I was a little boy, hearing my father [Hyrum Smith] sing. I do not know how much of a singer he was, for at that time I was not capable of judging as to the quality of his singing, but the hymns he sang became familiar to me even in the days of my childhood. I believe that I can sing them still, although I am not much of a singer."[1]

"I can remember, when I was a young boy, hearing my father [Joseph F. Smith] sing. I do not know how much of a singer he was, for at that time I was not capable of judging as to the quality of his singing, but the hymns he sang became familiar to me in the days of my childhood."[2]

---

1. Joseph F. Smith, in Conference Report, October 1899, pp. 68-69.

2. Joseph Fielding Smith, in Conference Report, October 1969, p. 110.

Spencer W. Kimball
In Our Lovely Deseret

I REMEMBER THE SONG "In Our Lovely Deseret," which Sister Eliza R. Snow wrote. She composed many of our songs. I can remember how lustily we sang:

> Hark! Hark! Hark! 'tis children's music —
> Children's voices, oh, how sweet,
> When in innocence and love,
> Like the angels up above,
> They with happy hearts and cheerful faces meet.[1]

I am not sure how much innocence and love we had, but I remember we sang it, even straining our little voices to reach the high E which was pretty high for children's voices. I remember we sang:

> That the children may live long
> And be beautiful and strong,

I wanted to live a long time and I wanted to be beautiful and strong — but never reached it.

> Tea and coffee and tobacco they despise,

And I learned to despise them. There were people in our rural community who were members of the Church who sometimes used tea and coffee and sometimes tobacco. The song goes on:

> Drink no liquor, and they eat
> But a very little meat;

(I still don't eat very much meat.)

> They are seeking to be great and good and wise.

---

1. *Hymns,* 1985, no. 307.

And then we'd "Hark! Hark! Hark" again,

> When in innocence and love,
> Like the angels up above,

And then the third verse went:

> They should be instructed young
> How to watch and guard the tongue,
> And their tempers train and evil passions bind;
> They should always be polite,
> And treat ev'rybody right,
> And in ev'ry place be affable and kind.

And then we'd "Hark! Hark! Hark" again. I was never quite sure whether the angels were limited in their voice culture as we were, but we were glad to take the credit.

In Conference Report, April 1978, pp. 70-71.

SPENCER W. KIMBALL
It Became a Part of My Life's Plan

FROM MY INFANCY I HAD HEARD the Word of Wisdom stories about tea and coffee and tobacco, etc. Nearly every Sunday School day and Primary day we sang lustily, I with the other boys,

> That the children may live long
> And be beautiful and strong,
> Tea and coffee and tobacco they despise,
> Drink no liquor, and they eat
> But a very little meat;
> They are seeking to be great and good and wise.

We sang it time and time again until it became an established part of my vocabulary and my song themes, but more especially my life's plan. Frequently fellows I knew sneaked out some tobacco or rolled their own on times like a 4th of July celebration. Some might even have had a sip from some man's liquor bottle.

These facts were drilled into me. Occasionally, some respected speaker said he had never tasted the forbidden things we sang against and then I made up my mind. Never would I use these forbidden things the prophets preached against. That decision was firm and unalterable. I would not and did not deviate.

In 1937 my wife and I were touring in Europe. In France I sat at a banquet table of the Rotary International Convention in a fashionable hotel. The large spacious banquet room held hundreds of people. The many waiters moved about the tables and at every place, besides plenteous silver, linen, and fancy serving dishes were seven wine glasses; at every plate seven different kinds of champagne, wine and every kind of liquor.

No one was watching me. Shall I drink it or at least sip it, the temptation nudged me. No one who cares will know. Here was quite a temptation. Shall I or shall I not?

Then the thought came: But I made a firm resolution when a boy that I would never touch the forbidden things. I had already lived a third of a century firm and resolute. I would not break my record now.

Address delivered at Thanksgiving Devotional, Salt Lake Valley seminary and institute students, 20 November 1977, pp. 10-12.

SPENCER W. KIMBALL
Don't Kill the Little Birds

ONE OF THE SONGS THAT HAS DISAPPEARED was number 163, "Don't Kill the Birds," and I remember many times singing with a loud voice:

> Don't kill the little birds,
> That sing on bush and tree,
> All thro' the summer days,
> Their sweetest melody.
> Don't shoot the little birds!
> The earth is God's estate,
> And he provideth food
> For small as well as great.[1]

I had a sling and I had a flipper. I made them myself, and they worked very well. It was my duty to walk the cows to the pasture a mile away from home. There were large cottonwood trees lining the road, and I remember that it was quite a temptation to shoot the little birds "that sing on bush and tree," because I was a pretty good shot and I could hit a post at fifty yards' distance or I could hit the trunk of a tree. But I think perhaps because I sang nearly every Sunday, "Don't Kill the Birds," I was restrained. The second verse goes:

> Don't kill the little birds,
> Their plumage wings the air,
> Their trill at early morn
> Makes music ev'rywhere,
> What tho' the cherries fall
> Half eaten from the stem?
> And berries disappear,
> In garden, field and glen?

---

1. *Deseret Sunday School Song Book* (Salt Lake City: Deseret Sunday School Union, 1908), no. 185.

This made a real impression on me, so I could see no great fun in having a beautiful little bird fall at my feet.

In Conference Report, Apr. 1978, p. 71.

DON'T KILL THE BIRDS.   185

1. Don't kill the lit-tle birds, That sing on bush and tree, All thro' the sum-mer
2. Don't kill the lit-tle birds, Their plumage wings the air, Their trill at ear-ly
3. Still like the widow's cruse, There's always plenty left; How sad a world were
4. Don't kill the lit-tle birds, That sing on bush and tree, All thro' the sum-mer

days, Their sweet-est mel-o-dy. Don't shoot the lit-tle birds! The
morn Makes mu-sic ev'-ry-where. What though the cher-ries fall half
this Of lit-tle birds be-reft. Think of the good they do in
days, Their sweetest mel-o-dy. In this great world of ours, if

earth is God's e-state, And He pro-vid-eth food For small as well as great,
eat-en from the stem? And ber-ries dis-ap-pear, In gard-en, field and glen?
all the orchards round; No hurt-ful in-sects thrive Where robins most a-bound.
we can trust His Word, There's food enough for all—Don't kill a sin-gle bird.

Deseret Sunday School Song Book (Salt Lake City: Deseret Sunday School Union, 1908), no. 185.

95

SPENCER W. KIMBALL AND EZRA TAFT BENSON

I Am a "Mormon" Boy

The twelfth and thirteenth presidents of the Church remember with fondness the Evan Stephens' song, "I Am a 'Mormon' Boy."

How proud I was when we were to sing in the congregation:

> A "Mormon" Boy, a "Mormon" Boy
> I am a "Mormon" Boy.
> I might be envied by a king,
> For I am a "Mormon" Boy.[1]

I liked this song; I have always gloried in those words: "I might be envied by a king, For I am a 'Mormon' Boy."[2]

President Benson has a great love for music and . . . has delighted audiences throughout the Church by singing, "I Am a Mormon Boy," a favorite song he learned in Primary.[3]

One such incident occurred in the Salt Lake Tabernacle on February 16, 1986, when the Saints of the Salt Lake Liberty and Salt Lake Monument Park stakes were assembled in regional conference. He remembered his Primary teacher had assigned him to sing a song for ward conference. He said he would never have had the courage to sing it were it not for his mother and his wonderful Primary teacher.

He then proceeded to sing all three verses of "I Am a 'Mormon' Boy."

---

1. *The Children Sing* (Salt Lake City: The Church of Jesus Christ of Latter-day Saints, 1951), no. 190.

2. Spencer W. Kimball, in Conference Report, April 1978, p. 71.

3. "First Year Was Full for Pres. Benson," *Church News,* 9 November 1986, p. 10.

No. 190   A Mormon Boy

EVAN STEPHENS   EVAN STEPHENS

1. Kind
2. I'm
3. My

friends, as here I stand to sing, So ver-y queer I feel, That
proud to know that I was born A-mong these mountains high, Where
fa-ther is a "Mor-mon" true, And when I am a man, I

now I've made my bow, I fear I don't look quite gen-teel; But,
I've been taught to love the truth, And scorn to tell a lie; Yet
want to be like him, and do Just all the good I can. My

The Children Sing (Salt Lake City: The Church of Jesus Christ of Latter-day Saints, 1951), no. 190.

97

A Mormon Boy

nev - er mind, for I'm a boy That's al - ways full of joy; A
I'll con - fess that I am wild, And oft - en do an - noy My
faults I'll try to o - ver - come, And while I life en - joy, With

rough and read - y sort of chap; An hon - est "Mor - mon" boy.
dear - est friends, but that's a fault Of many a "Mor - mon" boy.
pride I'll lift my head, and say, I am a "Mor - mon" boy.

A "Mor-mon" boy, a "Mor-mon" boy, I am a "Mor-mon" boy;

I might be en - vied by a king, For I am a "Mor-mon" boy.

EZRA TAFT BENSON
I Learned Every Word

I WAS ABOUT THIRTEEN YEARS OF AGE when father received a call to go on a mission. He went, leaving Mother at home with seven children. The eighth was born four months after he arrived in the field.

Mother was a stalwart. Never did we hear a murmur from her lips. The letters we received from Father were indeed a blessing. They seemed to us children to come halfway around the world, but they were only from Cedar Rapids, Marshall Town, Iowa; Chicago, Springfield, Illinois; etc. There came into our home, as a result, a spirit of missionary work that has never left it.

Father returned home and while we were sitting in the yard on one-legged milking stools, milking cows the "armstrong method," he would sing over and over again, "Ye Elders of Israel," "Israel, Israel, God Is Calling," "Come All Ye Sons of God," "Ye Who Are Called to Labor," until I learned every word of these great missionary songs. Today I don't need a songbook when we sing these great songs that Father sang to us morning and evening.

"A Boy from Whitney," *New Era*, November 1986, p. 28; used by permission.

Marion G. Romney
The Words of the Songs She Sang Comforted Me

As a child I lived in a land torn by a devastating revolution. As the contending forces pursued each other back and forth, I became greatly disturbed and agitated. Well do I remember when word came that the rebels were marching on Chihuahua City from Ciudad Juarez on the north and that the Federals were marching on the same city from Torreon on the south. My distress turned to fright—in fact, to terror—when they met at Casas Grandes, just ten miles away, and the shooting began. Some of our more adventuresome young men climbed to the top of the Montezuma Mountain where, through field glasses, they could watch the fighting.

Through those stirring and never-to-be-forgotten childhood experiences it was difficult for me to understand the doctrine of peace in one's heart while there was war in the land. But even then my fears were tempered some as I saw and listened to my sainted mother lull her babies to sleep. The words of the songs she sang comforted me. Some of them have been ringing in my mind through all the years of the intervening two-thirds of a century—these, for example, from "Guide Us O Thou Great Jehovah":

> When the earth begins to tremble,
> Bid our fearful thoughts be still;
> When thy judgments spread destruction,
> Keep us safe on Zion's hill.[1]

And these from Parley P. Pratt:

> Come, O thou King of Kings!
> We've waited long for thee,

---

1. *Hymns*, 1985, no. 83.

With healing in thy wings
To set thy people free.
Come, make an end to sin
And cleanse the earth by fire....[2]

And from W. W. Phelps:

In faith we'll rely on the arm of Jehovah
To guide thru these last days of trouble and gloom,
And after the scourges and harvest are over,
We'll rise with the just when the Savior doth come.[3]

---

2. *Hymns,* 1985, no. 59.

3. *Hymns,* 1985, no. 3.

"If Ye Are Prepared Ye Shall Not Fear," *Ensign,* July 1981, pp. 3-4; used by permission.

GORDON B. HINCKLEY
Praise to the Man

MANY YEARS AGO WHEN AT THE AGE of twelve I was ordained a deacon, my father, who was president of our stake, took me to my first stake priesthood meeting. In those days those meetings were held on a week night. I recall that we went to the Tenth Ward building in Salt Lake City. He walked up to the stand, and I sat on the back row, feeling a little alone and uncomfortable in that hall filled with strong men who had been ordained to the priesthood of God. The meeting was called to order, the opening song was announced, and—as was then the custom—we all stood to sing. There were perhaps as many as four hundred there. Together these men lifted their strong voices, some with the accents of the European lands from which they had come as converts, and all singing with a great spirit of conviction and testimony:

> Praise to the man who communed with Jehovah!
> Jesus anointed that Prophet and Seer.
> Blessed to open the last dispensation,
> Kings shall extol him, and nations revere.[1]

They were singing of the Prophet Joseph Smith, and as they did so there came into my young heart a great surge of love for and belief in the mighty Prophet of this dispensation. In my childhood I had been taught much of him in meetings and classes in our ward as well as in our home; but my experience in that stake priesthood meeting was different. I knew then, by the power of the Holy Ghost, that Joseph Smith was indeed a prophet of God.

---

1. *Hymns,* 1985, no. 27.

"Praise to the Man," *Ensign,* August 1983, p. 2; used by permission.

LeGrand Richards
Who's on the Lord's Side?

Out in the little country town where I was raised we used to have Sunday School conferences; I do not know whether we have them anymore. But I can remember a conference held there about eighty years ago when the visiting brethren from the Sunday School General Board were Brother Karl G. Maeser and Brother George Goddard. . . . I cannot remember to this day what Brother Maeser preached about in that conference, but I can remember old Brother George Goddard with his great singing voice and long beard, and I can remember the songs he taught us to sing in that conference. The first one — I do not think it is in the hymnbook anymore — went like this:

> Take away the whiskey, the coffee, and the tea,
> Cold water is the drink for me.

and then it repeats and goes on. That made such an impression upon me as a boy that I can hardly drink anything but cold water.

I was traveling on the train headed for Los Angeles a few years back, and I went into the diner for breakfast and the waiter said, "Are you ready for your coffee?"

"No, thank you."

"Would you like a glass of milk?"

"No, thank you."

"What do you want to drink?"

I said, "A glass of cold water, please."

He said, "You're the funniest man I ever did see."

The next song that Brother Goddard taught us to sing in that Sunday School conference (that was when I did not know that I could not sing, so I tried to sing with them) is still in the hymnbook. It goes like this:

Who's on the Lord's side? Who?
Now is the time to show,
We ask it fearlessly:
Who's on the Lord's side? Who?[1]

And, brothers and sisters, right there as a boy I resolved, the Lord being my help, that I'd try to be on his side as long as I lived.

---

1. *Hymns,* 1985, no. 260.

" 'Earth's Crammed With Heaven': Reminiscences," in *Devotional Speeches of the Year, 1977* (Provo: Brigham Young University Press, 1978), p. 155; used by permission.

DAVID B. HAIGHT
In Humility, Our Savior

I WISH EVERYONE COULD GROW UP IN a small town. I have so many happy memories of my boyhood. During those delightful summer and winter evenings we created most of our own activities and amusement. They were wonderful days. . . .

Sacrament meetings were very special occasions. . . . Everyone was expected to sing the special sacrament hymn. Everyone did sing. Children were trained not only to be reverent but to know some of the words of the most familiar sacrament songs. I can still see Sister Ella Jack, who led the music, standing in full view between the sacrament table and piano, as she would pause and look over the congregation to be sure everyone had a songbook and was ready to sing. She gave special attention to see that the Aaronic Priesthood boys had songbooks. We would all sing. We were learning in our youth that to feel of the Spirit we must experience a change in our hearts, and to be in harmony on this sacred occasion required our singing the sacrament hymns. As we personally sang the words, our souls were better prepared to understand this sacred ordinance. At the Last Supper, the early Apostles joined with the Savior in singing. Matthew records, "And when they had sung an hymn, they went out into the mount of Olives." (Matt. 26:30.)

And we would sing in that sacrament meeting . . .

> In humility, our Savior,
> Grant thy Spirit here, we pray;
> As we bless the bread and water
> In thy name this holy day.
> Let me not forget, O Savior,
> Thou didst bleed and die for me
> When thy heart was stilled and broken
> On the cross at Calvary.
> Fill our hearts with sweet forgiving;

Teach us tolerance and love.
Let our prayers find access to thee
In thy holy courts above.
Then, when we have proven worthy
Of thy sacrifice divine,
Lord, let us regain thy presence;
Let thy glory round us shine.[1]

These would be impressed upon our hearts because we had actually sung them. There come to one's soul heavenly thoughts as he joins in heavenly expressions coupled with heavenly melody.

---

1. *Hymns,* 1985, no. 172.

In Conference Report, April 1983, pp. 13-14; used by permission.

ARDETH GREENE KAPP
God Is with Thee

I HEAR YOUR MESSAGES, YOUNG WOMEN. I hear you with my ears and with my heart. I want to reach out to you and share with you what I have learned over the years about *hope*. I would give it to you if I could, but I've learned that it only comes from your own upward climb. You see, this brief time away from our heavenly home and parents is a time when we are given our agency for the purpose of being tried and tested in every way (see 2 Nephi 2:24-28). You should expect some "down" days and some hard tests. Learn from them. Grow from them. Be stronger because of them. Whenever I face things that I don't understand, I repeat in my mind the words of a song I learned years ago when I wondered if my prayers were being heard and I needed hope to carry on:

> In the furnace God may prove thee,
> Thence to bring thee forth more bright,
> But can never cease to love thee;
> Thou art precious in his sight.
> God is with thee, God is with thee;
> Thou shalt triumph in his might.[1]

---

1. *Hymns,* 1985, no. 43.

"A Time for Hope," *Ensign,* November 1986, pp. 87-88; used by permission.

LORIN F. WHEELWRIGHT
Our Parents Taught Us through Hymns

MY BROTHERS AND I LEARNED TO PLAY THE hymns as part of our piano lessons, and . . . learned to sing "I Am a 'Mormon' Boy." In our family, our mother carried a book of Deseret Sunday School Songs in the car. When we needed a change of attitude she started singing an appropriate hymn and she urged us to join with her. One of her favorites was "Let Us Oft Speak Kind Words to Each Other."

When we faced some personal trial, or a tough decision, or a performance test, we not only knelt in family prayer, but we also sang a comforting hymn. One that later echoed over and over in my mind as I lay in the hospital was "Jesus, My Savior True, Guide Me to Thee." And another that helped me resist the fiery darts of the adversary in a strange city far from home was "I Need Thee Every Hour." One of my father's favorite hymns was "School Thy Feelings." With it he taught us to strive to be longer suffering when our tempers flared.

"Let Us All Make a Joyful Sound," *Church News,* 27 August 1983, p. 7.

CAROLINE EYRING MINER
Singing Sermons

My mother [CAROLINE COTTAM ROMNEY EYRING[1]] knew almost every song in the hymn book by heart. She was not a talented singer, but she could carry a tune with enthusiasm and some accuracy, and she loved to sing. Sometimes, on a Sunday afternoon, she would gather us around the piano, which had known better days, and, starting with "Abide With Me," we would sing through to "Dear to the Heart of the Shepherd," which, as I remember, was in those days, the last song in the book.

"Count Your Many Blessings" was a favorite of Mother's, and she impressed its message upon us. There was never anyone who was more of an optimist than she. I often thought she was thankful that she didn't have anything except the spirit of being thankful. Now I know that is truly something to be thankful for.

"Angry Words! Oh, Let Them Never From the Tongue Unbridled Slip," we learned as a duet, and its message sank deep into my heart. Family harmony was a reality in more ways than one. "Do What Is Right . . . let the consequence follow" put the fearless militancy of the crusader into our hearts. It was Mother's father's favorite and exemplified his fearlessness well. We were rewarded with a dime each for learning the words of this magnificent hymn from beginning to end.

In our home evenings we usually sang "Love at Home," page forty-nine. It was easy to find and could be counted upon to set the proper mood. The words were then sung automatically, but the phrases come back to me again and again with renewed significance. "There is joy in every sound when there's love at home. . . . Oh, there's One who smiles on high when there's love at home."

"O My Father," with its plaintive melody and its bitter

---

1. Also the mother of Camilla Eyring Kimball, wife of Spencer W. Kimball; and Henry Eyring, internationally recognized scientist.

sweetness of sad associations at funerals was another song Mother loved to sing. The greatest favorite, though, was "There Is an Hour of Peace and Rest."

> There is an hour of peace and rest,
> Unmarred by earthly care;
> 'Tis when before the Lord I go,
> And kneel in secret prayer.
> May my heart be turned to pray,
> Pray in secret day by day. . . .[2]

These "sung sermons" have stayed with me much longer than the unsung ones, maybe because I was not conscious of their being sermons at all. By contrast, I tremble to think of the "sung sermons" some of our children are getting from television and radio without supervision. Maybe, as parents, we had better start singing more sermons of our own.

---

2. *Hymns,* 1985, no. 144.

"Singing Sermons," *Relief Society Magazine,* April 1962, p. 266; used by permission.

MARY JOHANSEN
Love, from Your Daughter Barbara

Even as a child I loved to sing. I would go into my room after church on Sunday and draw pictures and sing and sing, until my mother came to the door to say, "Mary, please don't sing so loud in there. It's not that we don't like to know you are happy, honey, but you know you just can't carry a tune."

Singing was in my heart, though, and I would go up into the woods behind our house and run through the woods singing all the songs I wanted to: Sad songs that broke my heart and I'd cry, and happy songs that made me feel so good I'd laugh out loud.

When I married and had my first child, I would sit and sing the loveliest songs to him. Songs I made up from my heart to tell him how much I loved him — how special he was to me. And he would smile and cuddle closer to me and fall asleep in my arms as I sang my songs of joy. Each child, then, received his or her own special song, made up just for that child, telling of my feelings and love for him. I sang only when there was no one around, for my husband agreed with my mother, "I'm sorry, honey, but you sound just awful when you sing."

The children didn't seem to mind my off-tune voice at all. In fact, we sang wonderful play songs together, laughing and playing and enjoying the sound of our voices. Many happy hours were spent sitting, marching, walking, and playing games with singsong instructions.

After having four wonderful children, I received my greatest joy — twin boys! What a blessing. How wonderful it was to sit and hold them in my arms for hours, singing of my love for them while they cuddled close to me and then fell asleep.

Because everyone had always told me that my singing voice left much to be desired, I hesitated to sing for anyone except the babies. In church, even though I knew the Lord loved to hear us sing, my "noise unto the Lord" was a very soft noise.

111

And at home I always made sure the house was empty before I picked up my hymnbook to sing my favorites.

One evening after the children had all gone to bed and my husband had duty at the Navy base, I picked up my hymnbook and began to sing "How Gentle God's Commands." I sang and felt the great love of our Heavenly Father who loves us so much even though we disregard his gentle commands. "O My Father," I sang, aching to go back to his home where I could be with him again. "The Lord Is My Light" — my favorite — I sang with all the love I felt in my heart for the guidance he had given me in my life.

Finishing my singing, I put my head in my arms and poured out my heart to my Heavenly Father, thanking him for the love he had for us, and for the great feeling of peace that came to me when I could sit and sing to him and talk to him, escaping from this mortal world for even a few minutes. Then I turned out the lights and went upstairs to my room. I noticed a sheet of paper on the dresser that hadn't been there before. I picked it up, and tears came to my eyes as I read:

Mom

I don't care what any one says about your singing voice. But I think it was so butiful the way you sang them songs. I was crying in my bed wile I was lisenning to you sing, and I love you very much.

love from your
daughter Barbara.

I found her with tears in her eyes in her bed. "Oh, Barbie," I said, "you are the only person who has ever told me he likes my singing. Thank you, honey." She hugged me back and sobbed. "Mommie, I just couldn't let it go. I had to get out of bed and write that note to you. I was crying listening to your beautiful singing."

I thought later that if our Heavenly Father loves my voice so much he inspires my daughter to write me a lovely note

112

and share her feelings with me, he must love to hear us sing more than I realize.

The next Sunday when we sang the opening song, I sang out just as loud as the rest of the people did. My Heavenly Father liked my voice, and that was all that mattered to me!

"Love, from Your Daughter Barbara," *Ensign*, December 1976, pp. 33-34; used by permission.

113

FIVE

GATHERING THE RIGHTEOUS WITH SONG

And whatsoever city thy servants shall enter, and the people of that city receive their testimony, let thy peace and thy salvation be upon that city; that they may gather out of that city the righteous, that they may come forth to Zion, . . . with songs of everlasting joy. (D&C 109:39.)

EDWARD TULLIDGE
Then Would Ring Out the Hymn of the Latter-day Saints

MUCH OF THE SUCCESS OF "MORMONISM" IN foreign lands is due to the fact that the elders, like Christ and his apostles of old, went about preaching the gospel "without purse or scrip." . . .

Though they bore the title of elders, these missionaries, especially the native ones, were generally young men from the age of twenty to thirty. Scarcely were they converted ere they were sent out to mission the land. . . .

Into the villages of England, Scotland, and Wales these youths made their way, with hymn-book and Bible in hand, but with no ministerial recommendation except a forceful, innovative intellectuality, and souls inspired with the glories of a new and conquering faith.

Alone, at eventide, they would uncover their heads, on some green bit of common, or, if on the Sabbath day, would daringly near the old village church, which well might tremble at such sacrilege, as did they literally in those bold missionary attempts, that never had been made but for youth's rich unconsciousness of inability. Then would ring out the hymn of the Latter-day Saints:

> Go, ye messengers of glory,
> Run, ye legates of the skies,
> Go and tell the pleasing story,
> That a glorious angel flies;
> Great and mighty,
> With a message from on high![1]

Or perchance it would be this instead:

---

1. *Latter-Day Saint Hymns* (Salt Lake City: Deseret Book, 1927), no. 48.

The morning breaks, the shadows flee;
Lo, Zion's standard is unfurled! . . .
The dawning of a brighter day
Majestic rises on the world.[2]

And many a village has been startled with this tremendous proclamation, from the lips of young men:

Jehovah speaks! Let earth give ear,
And Gentile nations turn and live.

First the woman would come out to listen, on the threshold of her cottage, after supper; then she would draw near, and wonder about this boy-preacher—to her eyes so much like her own boy, who, perhaps, is playing at some evening games with his companions, near by. Next comes her husband, and after awhile the boys themselves leave their games, and with their sisters, gather to listen. And so are also gathered other family groups of the village to swell the impromptu congregation. This is a truthful picture, for the author is describing a literal experience. . . .

'Tis a simple story; but from that house Mormonism is destined to spread through all the village, until the aged clergyman, educated at college, in his pulpit which he has occupied for a quarter of a century, fears that boy as much as a second Goliath might have feared the stripling David.

And thus Mormonism ran from village to town, and from town to city.

---

2. *Hymns,* 1985, no. 1.

The Women of Mormondom (New York: Tullidge & Crandall, 1877), pp. 268-72.

GEORGE ALBERT SMITH
Singing Softens Hearts

MANY YEARS AGO, TWO HUMBLE ELDERS laboring in the Southern States Mission were walking through the woods and finally came out into a clearing where there was a humble cottage, the home of friends who were not members of the Church. Overlooking this clearing was a hill covered by large trees. It had been a warm day, and when the elders arrived, instead of going into the house, they took their chairs out on the shady porch to visit with the family.

They didn't know that they were being watched or that danger threatened. They had come through a section of the country that was unfriendly, and having found a home where the family was friendly, they were grateful to the Lord for it.

They were asked to sing, and they selected the hymn, "Do What Is Right." And as they started to sing, there arrived on the brow of the hill above them a mob of armed horsemen. One of those men had previously threatened the missionaries and had kept watch for them on the road.

These armed men had come there with the determination to drive those missionaries out, but as they arrived at the top of the hill, they heard these missionaries singing. The leader of the mob dismounted and looked down among the trees and saw the roof of the house, but he could not see the elders. They continued to sing.

One by one the men got off their horses. One by one they removed their hats, and when the last note had died away and the elders had finished their singing, the men remounted their horses and rode away, and the leader said to his companions, "Men who sing like that are not the kind of men we have been told they are. These are good men."

The result was that the leader of the mob became converted to the Church and later was baptized. I never hear that hymn sung, but I think of that very unusual experience when two

119

missionaries, under the influence of the Spirit of God, turned the arms of the adversary away from them and brought repentance into the minds of those who had come to destroy them.

"The Power and Importance of Sincere Singing," *Improvement Era*, March 1951, pp. 141-42; used by permission.

MARVIN EARL BROWN
We're Going to Sing!

IN JUNE 1972 WHEN I WAS ATTENDING A Mission Presidents' Seminar prior to leaving for my mission in Argentina, I was privileged to interpret for President Benjamin Parra, who was the first non-English-speaking mission president ever called. It was at the final banquet that he arose to bear his testimony and related an experience he had had as a young missionary in Mexico. (I had heard of this young missionary through a mutual friend who had known him in the mission field. He was the grandson of one of the Mexican martyrs who was executed in 1912 by Pancho Villa for refusing to renounce his testimony. At the time of the execution, this martyr's wife was standing as a witness to it, holding a small child in her arms. This child had grown up to be the mother of President Benjamin Parra.)

As a young missionary, President Parra and his companion were riding on a train to go to a district conference where he, as a district president, would preside. As they rode through the night, he woke up his companion and said, "Levantese!" (Get up, get ready!) "Si, Parra." It was only about 4:00 in the morning but they got dressed. When the train stopped to pick up a can of milk, they jumped off the train. The companion then asked, "Que hacemos ahora, Parra?" (This was repeated every time the senior companion gave a little order.) "Que hacemos ahora, Parra?" (What are we going to do now?) "Caminamos!" (We're going to walk!) And they walked sixteen kilometers out across the desert through the bushes until they came to a hill. "Que hacemos ahora, Parra?" "Subimos" (We're going to climb!) And when they got to the top of this hill, "Que hacemos ahora, Parra?" "Cantamos!" (We're going to sing!) And they set their briefcases down, took out their hymnbooks, and sang four or five songs. The people from the village at the bottom of the hill gathered around them as they sang. They

121

preached to them for four or five hours, filled a ditch, and baptized the entire village. President Parra was guided by the Spirit to this distant village and gathered the people by singing the hymns.

Unpublished; used by permission.

MARJORIE P. HINCKLEY
Music Was the Missionary

On a beautiful Sunday morning in the fall of 1841, my great-grandfather, William Minshall Evans, then sixteen years of age, was walking down the streets of Liverpool, England, on his way to church. Suddenly he heard singing that thrilled him beyond anything he had ever heard before. He followed the sound down an alley and up some rickety stairs into a room where a few people were holding a meeting. John Taylor, who later became president of the Church and who had a beautiful voice, was the singer. The song he sang was so beautiful that William remained to hear the sermon.

Upon returning home, William was reprimanded by his elder brother, David, for being absent from his accustomed place in the choir. Asked to give an account of himself, William replied, "I have been where you should have been, and I shall not be satisfied until you all hear the wonderful truth I have heard this morning."

Before long, William and David were converted to the gospel, and then helped convert other members of their family. Three of the brothers and their parents emigrated to Utah between 1848 and 1850. William's mother died of cholera in Kanesville, Iowa, and her husband was so brokenhearted that he had no desire to continue on to Utah and so returned to England.

The boys experienced all of the hardships and trials of those early pioneer days, but remained true and faithful to the gospel. William had twelve children and passed on a great heritage to his posterity.

I[1] never sing the hymns of the Church without remembering that it was the singing of a hymn that opened the door

---

1. Marjorie P. Hinckley is the wife of Gordon P. Hinckley of the First Presidency of the Church.

to the gospel for my family and made it possible for me to enjoy all the blessings that have followed.

"Music Was the Missionary," *Ensign*, July 1981, p. 48; used by permission.

HARRY E. SNOW
Hymn Has Power

ON A WINDY DAY IN OCTOBER ABOUT two years ago, an elder turned away from a home in Columbus, Mississippi. As he left, a strong wind came up suddenly and blew some of his tracts out of his hand, carrying one of them around to the rear of the house where the gardener placed it in the trash can. Later, the sister of the housewife was looking through the can for a report thrown there by mistake. She came upon the tract with the words to "O My Father" written upon it.

She glanced at it and thrilled at the harmonious chord which it struck within her heart. Secretly she believed in her heart in some life before this yet did not know it as pre-existence. So fascinated with the poem was she that she sat down and memorized it before going into the house. Two years passed, during which she kept her treasured poem. She visited at the home of a friend whom she had previously advised not to rent rooms to Mormon elders.

Against her advice they had given the elders a room and on this afternoon, Miss Agnew sat on the front porch conversing with one of the elders. She asked to see the picture story of Mormonism and was astonished to find the poem "O My Father" written on the first page. She inquired into pre-existence and the resulting conversation lasted from four o'clock in the afternoon until far into the night. When she finally left, she had the answer to her question, "where did I come from."

From that time forward, she pursued a cautious study of Mormonism, mainly because of the curious fascination it held for her. She obtained a copy of the Book of Mormon intending to condemn it, but found nothing to condemn.

She accompanied the lady missionaries to the district conference where she was privileged to hear Elder Joseph F. Merrill and President William P. Whitaker. This she did at the risk of losing her position, but said later that it would have been well worth that sacrifice just to hear those two men speak.

Soon she will enter the waters of baptism and become a member of the Kingdom of God.

"Proselyting Tune," *Deseret News,* 15 February 1941, p. 9.

ERASTUS SNOW
Erastus the Singer

IN ONE OF THE WEALTHIER HOMES IN New Jersey lived a fine family, one who one day would touch the life of [Erastus Snow] very closely. The mother of the family was a regular churchgoer, a regular baptized church member. They were the cultured type of folk who would not have deigned to stop to listen to the harangue of a street vendor of the gospel. The father of the family alone did not wish to belong to any church for he didn't feel anything but irritation in the type of religion of the day. He did read his Bible and was willing that his wife be as active as she wished in her church and was more than willing that she teach her children the way of the good Lord Jesus.

This man, Nathaniel Ashby, was walking down the town's main thoroughfare one evening when he halted at the sound of a clear baritone voice coming from a hall down the street away. Stopping at the door he saw posted there a notice of a service being held there of the Church of Jesus Christ. Thinking to hear more singing, Nathaniel stepped inside just as the speaker bowed in prayer and how he prayed—"just as if the good Lord stood right at his side, not loud as if he needed to shout to make God hear his voice, but spoke as one man to another." Loving good music he was glad when the young man began another hymn, this one a favorite "I Need Thee Every Hour." For the first time he heard the story of the restored gospel, for the Elder (as you may have surmised) was [Erastus Snow]. Although he was only twenty-two years of age, he had preached many hundreds of sermons, had told the "glorious news" hundreds of times to many, many folks in these United States, and told it in such a way as to make those people think. Likely too, there had been a close connection between the close attention to his oratory, the subject matter told, and the contact with the soul he made with his singing.

When this same Nathaniel arrived home he explained to

his family that if they wanted to hear the hymns of the Church sung beautifully and the gospel story told convincingly, they had better go to that street the following Thursday. The sequel to this story was that the whole family was baptized.

Theresa Snow Hill, *Erastus Snow Stories* (Salt Lake City: Privately published, 1954), pp. 77-78.

MONTE M. DEERE, SR.
O God, the Eternal Father

Monte M. Deere Sr., a former University of Oklahoma football player, gets tears in his eyes when he hears or sings "O God, the Eternal Father."

The hymn, he said, helped lead to his conversion to the gospel. "I went to a sacrament meeting seventeen years ago at the invitation of Gary Cox, a Church member," he recalled. "Gary and I were instructor pilots at Vance Air Force Base in Oklahoma. We became good friends and often talked about religion. He invited me to go to Church.

"I felt a little out of place going to sacrament meeting that day. I had some of those 'first-time' type feelings and didn't know anyone except Gary. I sat about a third of the way down from the back of the chapel, way over on the left side. Since Gary was the branch president and was conducting the meeting, I sat alone.

"The sacrament hymn that Sunday was 'O God, the Eternal Father.' I was twenty-seven, and quite a tough fellow. I had never cried about anything in my life, but as I sat there listening to that hymn, I began crying. I wasn't sure what I was experiencing.

"Later, I told Gary about it and he explained that what I had felt was the Spirit bearing witness to me that the gospel was true. Gary and his wife and the missionaries began teaching me the gospel. I was baptized six weeks later and baptized my wife five years later."

Cox is now president of the Anchorage Alaska North Stake, and Deere is second counselor in the Norman Oklahoma Stake presidency.

"Hymns Bring Peace, Strength to Those in Need of Reassurance," *Church News*, 11 August 1985, pp. 7, 14.

PENNY ALLEN
He Isn't There

I'll try, but I don't think I can do it," I told the bishop over the telephone that morning. Usually, an invitation to sing is a happy opportunity, but he had asked me to sing at a funeral that afternoon, the funeral of a two-year-old boy who had suffocated in some dirt while at play.

The bereaved parents had asked the bishop to help with the funeral because the father had attended an LDS Sunday School for a while. That had been the extent of his contact with any church; but when trouble came, he reached back all those years to that source. The bishop had asked me to sing "O My Father," a song that always moved me to tears. As the mother of three small children, I was sentimental where children and helpless things were concerned. How could I sing that song—any song—on such an occasion?

But I had told the bishop I would try. I practiced at the organist's house, then we drove to the meetinghouse and met with the bishop for prayer in his office. I put off entering the chapel, but finally had to open the door. There, against a mass of gladiolas and palms, I saw a tiny, blue plush coffin. The scene blurred. I choked and lost control.

Then into my mind came the words "He isn't there." That was all. But the assurance that accompanied the words drove the lump from my throat and the tears from my eyes. I could sing.

I sang—not for the child who wasn't there, but for his parents who were there and needed to hear the message in that hymn. The bishop's sermon of reassurance and comfort visibly affected them. I remained calm, even when the mother half rose and gasped, "My baby . . ." as they carried the little coffin out.

The family joined the Church. I don't really know how the hand of the Lord worked in their conversion, but I do know that the message of the song was important enough that I could be calmed to sing it. As an echo of the angel's words at Jesus' tomb (see Matt. 28:6), the message of the words that had come into my mind has remained with me, and I have never forgotten it.

"He Isn't There," *Ensign*, July 1982, p. 41; used by permission.

WM. JAMES MORTIMER
Called to Serve

W HEN REGIONAL REPRESENTATIVES AND FULLTIME mission presidents met [in April 1985] during general conference, a simple event took place that will never be forgotten by those present.

The meeting itself was historic since it was the first time that all the mission presidents — those serving from around the world and those newly called who would begin service in July — and all of the Church's regional representatives had come together at one time.

But that is not what made the occasion so memorable.

The meeting in the Assembly Hall on Temple Square was filled with masterful discourses and important instructions from members of the First Presidency and the Council of the Twelve. The concluding speaker was Elder Boyd K. Packer, who had arranged the event that proved to be so profound.

Elder Packer spoke of missionary service and the importance of preparing to receive a mission call from the prophet. At an appointed moment about eighty young men and women from the Missionary Training Center entered the Assembly Hall from the rear, walking two by two, singing these words from a simple Primary song, "Called To Serve":

Called to serve Him, heav'nly King of glory,
Chosen e'er to witness for his name,
Far and wide we tell a Father's story,
Far and wide his love proclaim.
Onward, ever onward, as we glory in his name,
Onward, ever onward, as we glory in his name;
Forward, pressing forward, as a triumph song we sing.
God our strength will be; press forward ever,
Called to serve our King.[1]

---

1. *Hymns,* 1985, no. 249.

After walking through the aisles, the missionaries gathered in front of the rostrum and sang both this song again and "Carry On." Words were projected on a screen and the entire congregation joined in singing. The impact of this experience was so moving that tears were flowing and deep emotions were stirred. It was an unforgettable spiritual moment.

But why was it so memorable?

It was the impact of the music that really made the difference. The simple act of singing turned an otherwise fine meeting into a spiritually moving experience.

Good music is powerful!

"Music's Powerful Influence," *Church News,* 11 August 1985, p. 16.

DIANA MCFARLAND BROWN
Midnight Concert

IT WAS JUNE 1961, AND I WAS JOURNEYING with sixteen other students on a Brigham Young University travel study tour to study French in Quebec, Canada. We would be there tomorrow, and it was natural that our anticipation was mounting. As my anticipation grew, so did my apprehension: [for] the challenge I felt to be a missionary, an exemplar of gospel living. . . . At nineteen I had never really had any close associations with nonmembers. . . . it was difficult to speak of what I felt so deeply. . . .

"Let's go into the dome car and sing – practice some French songs and do some boning up," someone suggested.

We filed out of our car and into the connecting dome car. . . . We climbed the steps into the dome, and . . . found only two occupants, a young mother and her tearful little son. After the mother assured us that our singing would not disturb them, we began to sing, hesitantly and with much misuse of French accents and stumbling over words. Quickly our meager repertoire of French songs was exhausted, and we drifted comfortably into the familiar music and language of our Latter-day Saint hymns. It was comforting and strengthening to sing the hymns I'd sung since childhood, and I noticed the little boy stopped crying as we sang. Soon he fell asleep across his mother's lap.

I don't know how long we sang, but I recall the lifting of my spirit and the deepening of my conviction as we sang "I Know That My Redeemer Lives" and "O My Father," and the happiness we felt as we sang "Battle Hymn of the Republic." Finally, we ended with "Come, Come, Ye Saints," and as the last strains of "All is well" faded, we began to move quietly out of the dome.

I was first to leave the dome to descend to the lower level of the car, and I was unprepared for the sight that met my eyes. Dozens of upturned faces were looking toward us. Every

134

seat, which had been vacant when we entered the dome car earlier, was now filled, and the people were even standing and sitting in the aisles. Unknown to us, these people had gathered to listen as we sang. A woman standing near the stairway touched my arm, and I saw that there were tears in her eyes. "You young people sing so beautifully," she said, "because you sing from your hearts. Who are you, and where do you come from?"

"We're Mormons, ma'am," I replied. "We are students from Brigham Young University in Provo, Utah."

"Mormons . . . ," she murmured.

She was right. We had sung from our hearts, and my heart was still singing. I heard myself saying, "What do you know about the Mormons?"

"Well, I have heard your lovely Tabernacle Choir," she replied.

"Would you like to know more about the Mormons?" I asked.

"Yes, I really would."

"What do I do now?" I thought in panic. "I've finally asked the Golden Questions, but where do I begin?"

Then a calm, sure voice behind me spoke, and I turned to see a returned missionary from our group reach out and take the woman's hand in a warm, firm grasp. "Perhaps you have heard of a man named Joseph Smith," he said. "Let me tell you more about him."

Soon he was telling of Joseph Smith's first vision and explaining the coming forth of the Book of Mormon. Several people who had listened to us sing stayed to hear what this earnest young member of our group had to say, and some left their names and addresses with requests for missionary contact or for copies of the Book of Mormon.

I was filled with peace and joy. I had asked the Golden Questions, and my friend, the returned missionary, had shown me where to go from there. Only a short while before, we had sung about Joseph Smith's first vision in "Oh, How Lovely Was the Morning." From their earliest years in Primary, children in the Church hear the story of "the boy's first uttered prayer."

135

What better way to introduce the gospel than to relate that beautiful story? This experience was to guide me many times throughout the summer ahead.

In the years to come I was to learn to follow up the Golden Questions with an invitation to my home to see a film and meet the missionaries. And I have learned that there are many other effective ways to introduce the gospel to others. But I like to remember that night on the train when we sang from our hearts, unaware of our listeners. We truly did have something to sing about, and our message had been heard.

"Midnight Concert," *Ensign*, January 1981, pp. 28-30; used by permission.

SIX

I Am a Child of God

Lead me, guide me, walk beside me, Help me find the way.
Teach me all that I must do To live with him someday.
(Hymns, 1985, no. 301.)

NAOMI RANDALL
I Am a Child of God

DㄩRING GENERAL CONFERENCE IN APRIL 1957, Elder Harold B. Lee was put in charge of the dinner for the General Authorities and their wives. Elder Lee asked for a group of Primary children to sing. Young girls in costume sang, for the first time, a brand new song for children, "I Am a Child of God." Sister Naomi Randall, author of the poem, reports that when she heard them sing she knew that song was for every "child" of God around the world.

President David O. McKay, who was present, responded by saying, "O, little children of God, we will listen to your plea. We'll lead you, we'll guide you, we'll teach you, so that you may get back to your Father in Heaven with the help of General Authorities, the Priesthood, Relief Society, teachers, and parents.

"The children have shown us what our responsibility is. With the help of the Priesthood, and auxiliaries, we'll accept the challenge to listen to their plea."

Sister Randall continues, "This is one song that will live through eternity. I feel it began in the eternities. One little girl said she had heard and sung that song before. Perhaps she did, perhaps she did."

Handwritten memo of conversation with Robert L. Hales, 3 November 1976, Archives of The Church of Jesus Christ of Latter-day Saints; used by permission.

HAROLD B. LEE
A Mother's Teachings

THE IMPORTANCE OF TAKING ADVANTAGE OF EVERY hour of precious time allotted to each of us here was impressed forcibly upon me by an incident in my own family. A young mother came with her beautiful flaxen-haired six-year-old daughter to her grandparents. The mother asked if we would like to hear a beautiful new children's song which the daughter had just learned in her Primary class. While the little mother accompanied her, she sang:

> I am a child of God,
> And he has sent me here,
> Has given me an earthly home
> With parents kind and dear.
> I am a child of God
> And so my needs are great;
> Help me to understand his words
> Before it grows too late.
> I am a child of God,
> Rich blessings are in store;
> If I but learn to do his will
> I'll live with him once more.
> *Chorus:*
> Lead me, guide me, walk beside me,
> Help me find the way.
> Teach me all that I must do
> To live with him some day.[1]

Her grandparents were in tears. Little did they know then, that hardly before that little girl would have had the full opportunity for her mother to teach her all that she should know in order to return to her heavenly home, that [the] little mother

---

1. *Hymns,* 1985, no. 301.

would be suddenly taken away in death, leaving to others the responsibility of finding the answer to the pleadings of that childhood prayer, to teach and train and to lead her through the uncertainties of life.

What a difference it would make if we really sensed our divine relationship to God, our Heavenly Father, our relationship to Jesus Christ, our Savior and our elder brother, and our relationship to each other.

In Conference Report, October 1973, p. 9.

CAMILLA E. KIMBALL
We Are His Children

W<small>E HAD AN UNUSUAL EXPERIENCE IN THIS</small> recent journey that we have made. We had been visiting many of the less privileged members of the Church in the South Pacific and in the Caribbean area, where we have many new members. One experience that we had filled my heart with gratitude for what the gospel is doing for these dear people. We attended a meeting of the children in the school in the Samoan Islands. They have a Church school for the children there, and the students were gathered together on this particular occasion in the gymnasium, 1,700 little children. They were sitting on the floor just as close as they could get. It was wonderful to look out into the faces of these beautiful children with their black, shining eyes; and then to hear them sing "I Am a Child of God"; and to realize that beginning at the young age of kindergarten children up through the high schools they were being taught this wonderful hymn, that to me is one of the classic hymns of the Church.

> I am a child of God,
> And he has sent me here,
> Has given me an earthly home
> With parents kind and dear.
> Lead me, guide me, walk beside me,
> Help me find the way.
> Teach me all that I must do
> To live with him someday.[1]

To me, if we can have that in our hearts and our ambition, we will realize what a wonderful opportunity we have: We know where we came from. We know what the purpose of our life here is, and that is to grow and develop and to be useful and to advance in knowledge and in cultivating our

---

1. *Hymns,* 1985, no. 301.

142

talents, and then that we as women may have the wonderful opportunity and the privilege of being mothers in Israel and having the opportunity to teach little children to love our Heavenly Father and to know that we are his children and that he is so much concerned with us, each of us.

"We Are His Children," *New Era,* July 1981, p. 7; used by permission.

MARION D. HANKS
The Greatest Truth

[R]ECENTLY,] MY WIFE AND I WERE PRIVILEGED to visit Samoa and other islands in the far seas. One afternoon in the mountain tops of Upolu, in American Samoa, in the village of Sauniatu, we had a remarkable experience. . . . The village was deserted except for a few very young children and one or two who had stayed home with them. The rest were working in the fields or at other tasks. As we walked the single lane of Sauniatu, between the rows of *falés,* from the monument toward the new chapel and school, we heard children singing. There were perhaps half a dozen of them, none more than four years old, and they were singing with the sweetness of childhood a song we instantly recognized, and stood entranced, in tears, to hear: "I Am a Child of God."

In that high mountain fastness, at the end of a long, tortuous road, on an island of the sea, we found tiny dark-skinned children, none of them having seen more of the world than their small village, singing what they had learned through the tradition of their fathers, the greatest truth in existence, save one: I am a child of God.

That other truth? That there is a God who hears the voices of his children.

"The Tradition of Their Fathers," *Improvement Era*, December 1968, p. 97; used by permission.

144

FATHER OF SIX

A Song Awakened Me

7 October 1966

Dear Primary President:

I'm writing . . . anonymously but very gratefully and request that you forward it to the wonderful person who wrote the song titled "I Am a Child of God." . . . I am a professional officer in the Air Force, now stationed in Southeast Asia. All my life I have been active in the Church, missionary, stake mission president, stake MIA superintendent, etc.; but most recently a bishop. Now you might think that with this background a person would be so well intrenched that he would be quite impervious to weakness and temptation but it isn't so, as I can testify. You see, I thought about twenty months ago that I was going to war and requested my release as bishop of what was then thought to be two or three months prior to departure. So I was released — and the next day word arrived saying I was not going to Vietnam. Now came a period of inactivity for over a year and I found myself slipping in seeming small ways with my relationship. It seemed as though the Lord had drawn a dark curtain and shut me off from His spirit that had so constantly attended me before release. I think possibly the Lord was disappointed in me for quitting before necessary; at any rate, I was disappointed in myself.

With the spirit of darkness that hung over me I got so I not only couldn't pray but I couldn't care less. First to suffer from this was our home and family life. . . . Lots of things began to annoy me and then I stopped going to my Priesthood class. By the time I received orders to come over here I was fairly well on the road to total inactivity and who knows possible apostasy.

Three weeks ago I was awakened from sleep in a Bangkok hotel at 2:00 A.M. A song had awakened me and kept going

145

through my mind over and over. I tossed and turned and tried to turn it off but it wouldn't stop and then slowly I realized what the song was and started trying to recall the words. I'd never sung it but these words came to me: "Lead me, guide me, walk beside me, Help me find the way...." That was all. But what an impact! A swelling arose in my throat and tears sprang from my eyes ... and I was soon on my knees in humble prayer. Oh, how I poured out my heart to my Heavenly Father throughout the remainder of that night! I can't begin to tell you what peace and calm came over me, it was like going from night to day to once again feel the spirit of the Lord as a companion. To this day I have felt this presence every minute....

See what your song has done for me! I'm alive. I'm as happy as can be under the circumstances ... and somewhat useful again. And although we are a world apart, our home is closer knit than ever before ... and there "is joy in every sound."

I asked my wife to send me all the words to your song because it wouldn't leave me alone. Now I have the words and sing them several times daily while walking at camp or flying alone over the lonesome jungle. For the first time in my life I realize the full significance of the necessity to become as a little child if we would enter the Kingdom of Heaven. Although I'm approaching fifty, living under combat conditions and supposedly a hardened old veteran ... "I am a child of God."

Sincerely and gratefully yours,
A Father of Six

"I Am a Child of God," Original manuscript, Archives of The Church of Jesus Christ of Latter-day Saints; used by permission.

ROBERT L. SIMPSON
A Child's Song

I WAS TOUCHED BY THE STORY OF ONE highly successful business executive who recently responded graciously and humbly to a call to serve in his elders quorum presidency. Upon being asked the direct question: "What brought you back?" he responded, "Well, I have never told anyone before, but this is what happened: One morning while shaving, I overheard my six-year-old son singing from the next room. He was singing a little song I had heard him sing dozens of times before, 'I Am a Child of God'; but somehow that morning when he came to the part that says, 'Lead me, guide me, walk beside me, Help me find the way,' I had the feeling that he was singing directly to me. I just stood there and listened. Within seconds, my whole life seemed to pass in review; and it really came home with full force that some changes had to be made, especially when he came to the part, 'Teach me all that I must do, To live with him some day.'"

This good man confesses today that these simple words from the lips of his own child reached his heart as a personal plea. The plea was from a child of God who had been placed in his custody to be delivered back some day into Heavenly Father's presence. He concluded his answer to this question by stating that he decided then and there that he had something important to do, something more important than anything else in the world for a little fellow who still loved his daddy in spite of many personal failings.

In Conference Report, October 1969, p. 10; used by permission.

GARY LOREN MCCALLISTER
Song of Rescue

THE ACCIDENT OCCURRED AS WE WERE leaving town. . . . Our three-year-old daughter, G. J., was asleep in the back seat of our car, and we were anxious to return to our other three children. My wife, Gaydra, had begun to knit. Neither of us had reminded the other to fasten our seat belts. It was nearly five o'clock in the afternoon.

We were in heavy traffic moving at fifty-five miles an hour. As we approached an intersection, I suddenly saw a car that was coming from the opposite direction try to make a quick left turn in front of us. There was no way he could make it. And with cars on all sides of us, I couldn't turn. I slammed on the brakes.

The head-on collision threw me against the steering wheel and into the windshield. I began to gasp for air and tried to call Gaydra's name. I could see her on the floor, but she didn't answer me. . . . I could hear G. J. crying as I frantically kicked the collapsed steering wheel out of my lap. I was afraid the car might explode and felt I had to get my wife and daughter to safety.

At last the door was open and I stood up. The world began to turn white. . . . I regained consciousness as some men carried me to the grass at the side of the road. . . . I could still hear G. J. crying.

When the ambulance arrived, Gaydra and I and the other injured driver all rode on stretchers in the back. G. J. sat with a paramedic in the front of the ambulance. . . .

When we arrived at the hospital, G. J. had stopped crying. A doctor came into the emergency room and examined me. He gave the nurse instructions and left. She was pleasant but efficient: "Mr. McCallister, your wife has a depression fracture of the skull. It is causing severe pressure on her brain, and we are going to airlift her to the University Medical Center for

148

surgery. We can feel the loose bone. You are well enough that you can probably fly in the helicopter with her."

The nurse then left me alone. It was 5:20 by the clock on the wall, and the room was very quiet.

"Oh, Heavenly Father!" I cried. "Please help Gaydra. She can't die! She mustn't die!" . . . Those moments were the most agonizing of my life as I contemplated losing my eternal sweetheart.

Suddenly I became aware that someone was there at my side. Two men in street clothes, not white smocks, said hello. They were elders from the Church.

"Would you like a blessing?" one of them asked.

"Oh, yes. And my wife is in X ray. Please administer to her."

"We already have," they replied.

"My daughter . . . " I began.

"We've blessed her as well," the other man said.

They anointed my head with oil, gave me a blessing, and then left. It was 5:30 P.M.

I was puzzled. Who were those elders? *How* did they get there so fast?

Later I found out.

The twenty-year-old emergency paramedic driving the ambulance had his hands full. What was he to do with a three-year-old girl who was frightened and crying? Her parents were both injured, her mother critically. What could he say or do to calm this child?

Maybe a song would help, he thought. But he couldn't recall any children's songs — except one. It was a Sunday School song he had just learned in the church he had only recently joined. There was no reason this little girl would recognize it or take comfort in it. But the impression that he should sing grew stronger, so he began: "I am a child of God, and he has sent me here . . . "

The little girl grew quiet and after a verse began to sing with him, "I am a child of God, and so my needs are great . . . "

At the end of the second verse he asked softly, "Are you a Latter-day Saint?"

She replied, "Yes."

"Are your mommy and daddy?"

"Yes."

He reached for the radio transmitter. "This is rescue calling base. Hi, Beth. Hey, would you do me a favor? Look up the number of a Bishop Brower in the phone book and give him a call. We have a critically injured woman coming in who's a member of his church and we need . . . "

So the bishop received the message, and the priesthood holders were at the hospital within minutes.

Gaydra was never flown to the medical center. They couldn't find the fracture in X ray. G. J. and I were released that night, and two weeks later we took Gaydra home without surgery. Except for an inability to recall the accident and the several days following, she has totally recovered. We had survived a head-on collision at fifty-five miles an hour.

A year later we attended the missionary farewell of the young paramedic who helped save Gaydra's life.

"Song of Rescue," *Ensign*, July 1985, pp. 48-49; used by permission.

SEVEN

COME, COME, YE SAINTS

We'll make the air with music ring, Shout praises to our God and King; Above the rest these words we'll tell—All is well! All is well! (Hymns, *1985, no. 30.)*

JOSEPH FIELDING SMITH
Prayer and Love of God

Now, IN THIS . . . SONG, "All is Well," is a familiar household song with us, but to my mind the inspiration, the beauty and strength of this song will some day make it prized as one of the gems of American literature. . . .

What a magnificent outpouring of the human soul that song is! When you think of a band of people, driven from the confines of civilization, and facing the necessity of thousands of miles of travel to an unknown, new world, with all the deprivation and hardship such an undertaking would entail, to my mind the expression — and it was a true expression of the spirit of the people who composed that great band — is one of the finest utterances of the human soul.

"Prayer and Love of God," Journal History of the Church, 10 September 1933, Archives of The Church of Jesus Christ of Latter-day Saints, p. 6.

LDS MISSIONARY
Saved by a Song

As THE LAST FAINT STREAK OF PARTING DAY was softly fading across the western skies, four missionaries appeared on a street corner in a little Oklahoma Indian village. They opened their street meeting by singing the famous Mormon hymn, "Come, Come, Ye Saints." As they finished singing this song, an old Indian Chief, bent and wrinkled by many moons, pushed to the front and listened to the message of the missionaries. At the close of the meeting he invited the missionaries to his hogan or tee-pee. He asked them to be seated, as he took from behind the door an old violin. He said: "The song you sang tonight is my song. I will play you the same song and tell you the story of your forefathers and this song.

"Many, many moons ago, my people were on the war path. We hated the palefaces. We held council and decided to kill every one. A band of palefaces were going west. They had almost reached the Rocky Mountains. I was the Chief of one thousand young braves. That night, silently we waited on a mountain pass for these people, which were led by Brigham Young. There were braves with bow and arrows behind every rock and tree, waiting to pounce down upon the palefaces.

"The Pioneers camped for the night and prepared supper. The big bonfire was burning brightly and the palefaces danced around the fire. Everyone then sat down and began singing 'Come, Come, Ye Saints.' I gave the signal, but our fingers were like stone. Not one arrow was shot. We mounted our horses and rode back to camp. We knew the great Spirit was watching over the palefaces.

"This is your song. It was your forefathers' song and it is my song every night before I go to bed. It brings the great Spirit here to me and makes me and my people happy."

Marilyn Pully, "Saved by a Song," *Children's Friend*, July 1942, p. 319; used by permission.

OSCAR WINTERS
We Dug a Shallow Grave

ONE NIGHT, AS WE WERE MAKING CAMP, we noticed one of the brethren had not arrived, and a volunteer party was immediately organized to return and see if anything had happened to him. Just as we were about to start, we saw the missing brother coming in the distance. When he arrived he said he had been quite sick; so some of us unyoked his oxen and attended to his part of the camp duties.

After supper, he sat down before the campfire on a large rock, and sang in a very faint but plaintive and sweet voice, the hymn, "Come, Come, Ye Saints." It was a rule of the camp that whenever anybody started this hymn all in the camp should join; but for some reason, this evening nobody joined him; he sang the hymn alone. When he had finished, I doubt if there was a single dry eye in the camp.

The next morning we noticed that he was not yoking up his cattle. We went to his wagon and found that he had died during the night. We dug a shallow grave, and after we had covered his body with the earth we rolled the large stone to the head of the grave to mark it, the stone on which he had been sitting the night before when he sang: "And should we die before our journey's through, happy day! All is well!"

Heber J. Grant, "Favorite Hymns," *Improvement Era*, June 1914, pp. 781-82; used by permission.

BOYD K. PACKER
It Was as Though the Engines Would Sing Back to Me

I HAVE A BROTHER WHO BECAME A brigadier general in the Air Force. During World War II he was a bomber pilot and took part in some of the most dangerous and desperate raids in Europe. He returned to an assignment in Washington, D.C., about the time I finished pilot training in the same B-24 bombers and was heading for the Pacific. We had a day or two together in Washington before I left for overseas.

We talked of courage and of fear. I asked how he had held himself together in the face of all that he had endured.

He said, "I have a favorite hymn — 'Come, Come, Ye Saints,' and when it was desperate, when there was little hope that we would return, I would keep that on my mind and it was as though the engines of the aircraft would sing back to me:"

> Come, come, ye Saints,
> No toil nor labor fear;
> But with joy wend your way.
> Though hard to you
> this journey may appear,
> Grace shall be as your day.[1]

From this he clung to faith, the one essential ingredient to courage.

There are many references in the scriptures, both ancient and modern, that attest to the influence of righteous music. The Lord, Himself, was prepared for His greatest test through its influence, for the scripture records: "And when they had sung an hymn, they went out into the mount of Olives." (Mark 14:26.)

I bear witness that God is our Father, that we are His children, that He loves us and has provided great and glorious

---

1. *Hymns*, 1985, no. 30.

things in this life. I know this, and I thank Him for the uplifting influence of good music in my life and in the lives of my children. There are many things we can do together as a family; inspired music we can feel together. In the name of Jesus Christ. Amen.

In Conference Report, October 1973, p. 25; used by permission.

EZRA TAFT BENSON

No Strains of Music Were Ever More Welcome

Shortly after the close of World War II, Elder Ezra Taft Benson was assigned to be the president of the European Mission. Among his duties was the distribution of food and clothing from the Church in America. He traveled to Europe with Frederick W. Babbel, who gives the following account of how a famous hymn led them to the assembled saints.

UPON ARRIVING AT KARLSRUHE, WE MADE inquiries to learn where our saints might be meeting in district conference. Finally, there was pointed out to us a sizeable area of almost completely demolished buildings and we were told that they were probably meeting somewhere in that section.

Parking our car near massive heaps of twisted steel and concrete, we climbed over several large piles of rubble and threaded our way between the naked blasted walls in the general direction which had been pointed out to us. As we viewed the desolation on all sides of us, our task seemed hopeless. Then we heard the distant strains of "Come, Come, Ye Saints" being sung in German. We were overjoyed. No strains of music were ever more welcome!

We hurried in the direction of the sound of the singing and arrived at a badly scarred building which still had several usable rooms. In one of the rooms we found 260 joyous saints still in conference, although it was already long past their dismissal time. (They had already been in session over three hours that afternoon, but had been hoping and praying that we might arrive in time to meet with them.)

As we entered the room, the closing strains of this beloved Mormon hymn swelled to a crescendo of joyousness that overwhelmed us. . . .

With tears of gratitude streaming down our cheeks, we

went as quickly as possible to the improvised stand. Never have I seen President Benson so deeply and visibly moved as on that occasion. . . . The entire audience rose to its feet to pay silent tribute to President Benson and to get a better look at us as we moved to the front. . . . In a moment, President Benson arose and [delivered a speech].

Frederick W. Babbel, *On Wings of Faith* (Salt Lake City: Bookcraft, 1972), pp. 36-37; used by permission.

CALVIN R. BROWN
The Song Changed My Life

I FIRST JOINED THE MORMON TABERNACLE CHOIR in 1944 at age 17. A year later I found myself in Bremen, Germany, a 2nd Lt. in the U. S. infantry. One Sunday morning during Christmas, I was alone by the great Dom in downtown Bremen, viewing with horror the total destruction of that beautiful city. Suddenly I heard the unmistakable strains of "Come, Come, Ye Saints" in German drifting across the bombed out ruins.

With great nostalgia and anticipation, I followed the sounds up some creaky stairs to a Sporthalle behind the great cathedral. When I opened the door, the singing stopped as all faces turned to me, noticing my uniform.

Having experienced the most severe persecution all through the war, they were obviously frightened by my appearance. I tried to calm them and then began speaking in what they described as "German without accent." It must have been the gift of tongues. They considered me some kind of messenger delivering them from the extended period of darkness that they had suffered under Hitler. We then sang "Come, Come, Ye Saints" together. I never hear it sung without remembering those tearful faces that day. The song changed my life.

Paul E. Dahl, " 'All Is Well . . .': The Story of 'the Hymn That Went around the World'," in *BYU Studies*, Winter 1981 (Provo: Brigham Young University Press, 1981), p. 526.

ORSON H. TAYLOR
A Time of Renewal

I MET HIM IN PALO ALTO, CALIFORNIA. He explained that he was a member of The Church of Jesus Christ of Latter-day Saints, and when he discovered that I also was a Latter-day Saint, he told me this story.

In the early days of the Church his father was sent as one of the first missionaries to Turkey. He spent eight years there, most of them in prison. By the time he escaped and returned to America, he had changed, and this rebellious son could not understand his strict father. So he left home.

Years later, in a hotel room, after emptying a bottle of liquor, he snapped on the radio to hear the war news. Instead, there came loud and clear the beautiful strains of "Come, come ye Saints, no toil nor labor fear," from a Tabernacle Choir broadcast.

He stood transfixed. As the tones swelled forth, his heart swelled too, until he thought it would burst. He remembered his parents begging him not to leave them. His life passed before him, and he shook with a great and unusual pain. Tears came in torrents.

When his emotions had subsided, he bathed and put on clean clothes and went to the nearest LDS chapel. There he took the bishop's hand in both of his and said, "I want you to be a witness for a new covenant I made with my Father in heaven. In my life from now on I will put evil behind me and strive to build up the kingdom here on earth."

He never broke that covenant.

"A Time of Renewal," *Ensign,* April 1974, p. 35; used by permission.

Susan Linford
Gird Up Your Loins!

While serving a mission in South America, I had the experience that almost every missionary has—having to get along with a companion who is very difficult to get along with. To make matters worse, at the time I received this new companion, I had been suffering from minor illnesses which were hard to control because medication was not readily available and the daily 110 degree heat seemed to intensify my discomfort. The missionary work in the city in which we were located progressed at a painstakingly slow rate. The added pressure for baptisms seemed weightier than ever and it was easy to become discouraged when the people were not interested in what we had to give them.

I remember one day in particular when I was waiting with my companion for a meeting in the chapel. I was so discouraged and unhappy. I felt like my life was so hard and I did not know how I was going to live through it. I could not keep the tears from welling up in my eyes. It happened to be July 24th in a country where there is no regard given to such an important date of celebration in our Church. Thinking of this brought on more homesickness and an even deeper yearning to find a remedy for my miserable state.

As I sat waiting in the chapel with nothing better to do than drown myself in my sorrows and self-pity, I picked up a hymn book. I happened to turn to "Come, Come, Ye Saints." My tear-filled eyes slowly read through the first verse. Then, as I read the second verse, my whole soul was struck powerfully with the true meaning William Clayton expressed in these humble words:

> Why should we mourn or think our lot is hard?
> 'Tis not so; all is right.
> Why should we think to earn a great reward
> If we now shun the fight?

Gird up your loins; fresh courage take.
Our God will never us forsake;
And soon we'll have this tale to tell —
All is well! All is well![1]

This made such an impression on me. What a blessing it was to read those inspiring words of encouragement at such a time in my life!

Now, when I think back on this experience, I have to chuckle at myself for thinking I had it so bad when I really didn't at all. But how grateful I was for this beautiful hymn which helped me to put my problems in a more appropriate perspective.

---

1. *Hymns,* 1985, no. 30.

Unpublished; used by permission.

JEFFREY R. HOLLAND
All Is Well!

SEVERAL DECADES AGO AN ACQUAINTANCE OF mine left a small southern Utah town to travel to the East. He had never traveled much beyond his little hometown and certainly had never ridden a train. But his older sister and brother-in-law needed him under some special circumstances and his parents agreed to free him from the farm work in order to go. They drove him to Salt Lake City, and put him onto the train — new Levi's, not so new boots, very frightened, and eighteen years old.

There was one major problem and it terrified him. He had to change trains in Chicago. Furthermore, it involved a one-night layover, and that was a fate worse than death. His sister had written, carefully outlining when the incoming train would arrive and how and where and when he was to catch the outgoing line, but he was terrified.

And then his humble, plain, sun-scarred father did something no one . . . should ever forget. He said, "Son, wherever you go in this Church, there will always be somebody to stand by you. That's part of what it means to be a Latter-day Saint." And then he stuffed into the pocket of his calico shirt the name of a bishop he had taken the time to identify from sources at Church headquarters. If the boy had troubles, or became discouraged and afraid, he was to call the bishop and ask for help.

Well, the train ride progressed rather uneventfully until it pulled into Chicago. And even then the young man did pretty well at collecting his luggage and making it to the nearby hotel room that had been prearranged by his brother-in-law. But then the clock began to tick and night began to fall and faith began to fail. Could he find his way back to the station? Could he find the right track and train? What if it was late? What if he was late? What if he lost his ticket? What if his sister had made a mistake and he ended up in New York? What if? What if? What if?

164

Without those well-worn boots ever hitting the floor, that big, raw-boned boy flew across the room, nearly pulled the telephone out of the wall, and, fighting back tears and troubles, called the bishop. Alas, the bishop was not home, but the bishop's wife was. She spoke long enough to reassure him that absolutely nothing could go wrong that night. He was, after all, safe in the room, and what he needed more than anything else was a night's rest. Then she said, "If tomorrow morning you are still concerned, follow these directions and you can be with our family and other ward members until train time. We will make sure you get safely on your way." She then carefully spelled out the directions, had him repeat them back, and suggested a time for him to come.

With slightly more peace in his heart, he knelt by his bed in prayer (as he had every night of his eighteen years) and then waited for morning to come. Somewhere in the night, the hustle and bustle of Chicago in the 1930s subsided into peaceful sleep.

At the appointed hour the next morning, he set out. A long walk, then catch a bus. Then transfer to another. Watch for the stop. Walk a block, change sides of the street, and then one last bus. Count the streets carefully. Two more to go. One more to go. I'm here. Let me out of this bus. It worked, just like she said.

Then his world crumbled, crumbled before his very eyes. He stepped out of the bus onto the longest stretch of shrubbery and grass he had ever seen in his life. She had said something about a park, but he thought a park was a dusty acre in southern Utah with a netless tennis court in one corner. Here he stood looking in vain at the vast expanse of Lincoln Park with not a single friendly face in sight.

There was *no* sign of a bishop or ward or meetinghouse. And the bus was gone. It struck him that he had no idea where he was or what combination of connections with who knows what number of buses would be necessary to get him back to the station. Suddenly he felt more alone and overwhelmed than at any moment in his life. As the tears welled up in his eyes, he despised himself for feeling so afraid—but he was, and the tears would not stop. He stepped off the sidewalk away from the bus stop into the edge of the park. He needed some privacy for his tears, as only an eighteen-year-old from southern Utah could fully appreciate. But as he stepped away from the noise, fighting to control his emotions, he thought he heard something hauntingly familiar in the distance. He moved cautiously in the direction of the sound. First he walked, and then he walked quickly. The sound was stronger and firmer and certainly it was familiar. Then he started to smile, a smile which erupted into an audible laugh, and then he started to run. He wasn't sure that was the most dignified thing for a newcomer to Chicago to do, but this was no time for discretion. He ran, and he ran fast. He ran as fast as those cowboy boots would carry him — over shrubs, through trees, around the edge of a pool.

> Though hard to you this journey may appear,
> Grace shall be as your day.

The words were crystal clear, and he was weeping newer, different tears. For there over a little rise huddled around a few picnic tables and bundles of food was the bishop and his wife and their children and most of the families of that little ward. The date: July 24, 1934. The sound: a slightly off-key, a capella rendition of lines that even a boy from southern Utah could recognize.

> Gird up your loins; fresh courage take.
> Our God will never us forsake;
> And soon we'll have this tale to tell —
> All is well! All is well!

It was Pioneer Day. The gathering to which he had been invited was a twenty-fourth of July celebration. Knowing that it was about time for the boy to arrive, the ward had thought it a simple matter to sing a verse or two of "Come, Come, Ye Saints" to let him know their location.

"Are You True?" in *Devotional Speeches of the Year, 1980* (Provo: Brigham Young University Press, 1981), pp. 43-45; used by permission.

Hymn Index

Hymns and songs referred to in this collection of stories are listed below with a reference to the book in which they were most recently published.

Eugene England, "Welded Together in Spiritual Unity and Power and Beauty," 70

How Firm a Foundation (*Hymns,* 1985, no. 85): Kathryn Wouden, "The Old Man Who Sang," 29-32; Amanda Smith, "I'll Never, No Never, No Never Forsake," 50-51; Vessa McGrath, "When through the Deep Waters," 52; Wm. James Mortimer, "It Still Gives Me Strength," 53; W. Herbert Klopfer, "My Heart Was Touched," 54-55

How Gentle God's Commands (*Hymns,* 1985, no. 125): Ardeth G. Kapp, "How Gentle God's Commands," 74-75; Mary Johansen, "Love, from Your Daughter Barbara," 111-13

How Great Thou Art (*Hymns,* 1985, no. 86), Vera N. Forsyth, "Music Brought Me Comfort," 18

I Am a Child of God (*Hymns,* 1985, no. 301): Marion D. Hanks, "I Began To Sing a Song," 4; Kathryn Wouden, "The Old Man Who Sang," 29-32; Neal A. Maxwell, "I Remember What We Sang," 58; Jay Criddle Hess, "The Hymns Provided Me with the Greatest Lessons," 59-60; Naomi Randall, "I Am a Child of God," 139; Harold B. Lee, "A Mother's

Teachings," 140-41; Camilla E. Kimball, "We Are His Children," 142-43; Marion D. Hanks, "The Greatest Truth," 144; Father of Six, "A Song Awakened Me," 145-46; Robert L. Simpson, "A Child's Song," 147; Gary Loren McCallister, "Song of Rescue," 148-50

I Am a "Mormon" Boy (*The Children Sing,* 1951, no. 190): Spencer W. Kimball, "I Am a 'Mormon' Boy," 96-98; Ezra Taft Benson, "I Am a 'Mormon' Boy," 96-98; Lorin F. Wheelwright, "Our Parents Taught Us through Hymns," 108

I Know That My Redeemer Lives (*Hymns,* 1985, no. 136): Jerry Borrowman, "You're the Future of the World," 27-28; Robert L. Simpson, "Effect of Church Hymns," 82; Diana McFarland Brown, "Midnight Concert," 134-36

I'll Go Where You Want Me to Go (*Hymns,* 1985, no. 270): Yoshihiko Kikuchi, "I'll Go Where You Want Me to Go," 7-8; Melvin J. Ballard, "Words of Comfort," 9-10; Louisette Castonguay, "Tears Started Flowing," 11

I Need Thee Every Hour (*Hymns,* 1985, no. 98): Spencer W. Kimball, "I Need Thee Every Hour," 71; Spencer W. Kimball,

170

171

Author Index

174

175

Title Index

Subject Index

Activity

Ezra Taft Benson, "When I Was Called as a Scoutmaster," 67-68

Aesthetic Experience

Eugene England, "Welded Together in Spiritual Unity and Power and Beauty," 70

Animals

Spencer W. Kimball, "Don't Kill the Little Birds," 94-95

Beauty

Eugene England, "Welded Together in Spiritual Unity and Power and Beauty," 70

Blessings from Singing

Paul N. Davis, "Preparing Myself Spiritually to Give a Patriarchal Blessing", 77-79; Marvin Earl Brown, "We're Going to Sing!" 121-22

Boy Scouts

Ezra Taft Benson, "When I Was Called as a Scoutmaster," 67-68

Cheer, Good

W. Herbert Klopfer, "My Heart Was Touched," 54-55

Comfort

Marion D. Hanks, "I Began To Sing a Song," 4; Melvin J. Ballard, "Words of Comfort," 9-10; Lorin F. Wheelwright, "Our Parents Taught Us through Hymns," 16-17; Vera N. Forsyth, "Music Brought Me Comfort," 18; Kathryn Wouden, "The Old Man Who Sang," 29-32; Amanda Smith, "I'll Never, No Never, No Never Forsake," 50-51; Hugh W. Pinnock, "The Singing of Hymns Had Saved the Day," 81; Marion G. Romney, "The Words of the Songs She Sang Comforted Me," 100-101; Ardeth G. Kapp, "God Is with Thee," 107

Comfort — Bereavement

Connee Garrett, "Hold to the Rod," 15; Vessa McGrath, "When through the Deep Waters," 52; Penny Allen, "He Isn't There," 130-31

Comfort — Death

Joseph Smith, "A Poor Wayfaring Man of Grief," 36-37; Jane Paskett Judd, "I Would Like to Sing," 40

181

Familiar to Me," 89; Mary Johansen, "Love, from Your Daughter Barbara," 111-13; George Albert Smith, "Singing Softens Hearts," 119-20; Marvin Earl Brown, "We're Going to Sing!" 121-22

Identification of Fellow Saints

Colleen C. Evans, "Fear Not, for the Lord Is on Our Side," 23; W. Herbert Klopfer, "Fellowship with the Saints through the Tune of a Hymn," 56-57; Neal A. Maxwell, "I Remember What We Sang," 58; Gilbert Scharffs, "The Elder Began to Whistle," 61-63; Marion D. Hanks, "The Greatest Truth," 144; Gary Loren McCallister, "Song of Rescue," 148-50; Ezra Taft Benson, "No Strains of Music Were Ever More Welcome," 158-59; Orson H. Taylor, "A Time of Renewal," 161; Jeffrey Holland, "All Is Well!" 164-66

Influence

Ezra Taft Benson, "When I Was Called as a Scoutmaster," 67-68; Hugh W. Pinnock, "The Singing of Hymns Had Saved the Day," 81; Joseph F. Smith, "The Hymns He Sang Became Familiar to Me," 89; Joseph Fielding Smith, "The

Hymns He Sang Became Familiar to Me," 89; Wm. James Mortimer, "Called to Serve," 132-33

Influence — Childhood

Joseph F. Smith, "The Hymns He Sang Became Familiar to Me," 89; Joseph Fielding Smith, "The Hymns He Sang Became Familiar to Me," 89; Spencer W. Kimball, "In Our Lovely Deseret," 90-91; Spencer W. Kimball, "It Became a Part of My Life's Plan," 92-93; Spencer W. Kimball, "Don't Kill the Little Birds," 94-95; Spencer W. Kimball, "I Am a 'Mormon' Boy," 96-98; Ezra Taft Benson, "I Learned Every Word," 99; Gordon B. Hinckley, "Praise to the Man," 102; LeGrand Richards, "Who's on the Lord's Side?" 103-4; David B. Haight, "In Humility, Our Savior," 105-6; Orson H. Taylor, "A Time of Renewal," 161

Influence — Parental

Vessa McGrath, "When through the Deep Waters," 52; Hugh Pinnock, "The Singing of Hymns Had Saved the Day," 81; Ezra Taft Benson, "I Learned Every Word," 99; Marion G. Romney, "The Words of the Songs She

185

Alice Washburn, "Still Singing by My Side," 14; Naomi Randall, "I Am a Child of God," 139

Obedience

Yoshihiko Kikuchi, "I'll Go Where You Want Me to Go," 7-8; Alice Washburn, "Still Singing by My Side," 14; Ardeth G. Kapp, "How Gentle God's Commands," 74-75

Packer, Boyd K.

Wm. James Mortimer, "Called to Serve," 132-33

Parental Example. *See* Example, Parental

Peace

Melvin J. Ballard, "Words of Comfort," 9-10; Paul Sutorius, "Peace — If Not Plenty — Here Abides," 24-25; Mary Johansen, "Love, from Your Daughter Barbara," 111-13

Perfection, Striving for

Boyd K. Packer, "The Inspiration of Sacred Music," 73

Pioneers

Eliza R. Snow, "The Glory of God Seemed to Rest on All," 38-39; Jane Pasket Judd, "I Would Like to Sing," 40; LDS

Missionary, "Saved by a Song," 154

Power

W. Herbert Klopfer, "Fellowship with the Saints through the Tune of a Hymn," 56-57

Prayer

Rex D. Pinegar, "Did You Think to Pray?" 3; Melva Lee Wheelwright, "My First Night Alone," 16-17; Richard Rust, "Hymn of Comfort," 21-22; Wm. James Mortimer, "It Still Gives Me Strength," 53

Primary Songs

Marion D. Hanks, "I Began To Sing a Song," 4; Naomi Randall, "I Am a Child of God," 139; Harold B. Lee, "A Mother's Teachings," 140-41

Protection

Ezra T. Benson, "A Song for a Lion," 41; Boyd K. Packer, "The Inspiration of Sacred Music," 73; George Albert Smith, "Singing Softens Hearts," 119-20

Pyper, George D.

Melvin J. Ballard, "Words of Comfort," 9-10

Reactivation

Robert L. Simpson, "Effect of Church Hymns," 82; Robert

187

Kimball, "Don't Kill the Little Birds," 94-95; David B. Haight, "In Humility, Our Savior," 105-6; Lorin F. Wheelwright, "Our Parents Taught Us through Hymns," 108; Caroline Eyring Miner, "Singing Sermons," 109-10; Naomi Randall, "I Am a Child of God," 139; Harold B. Lee, "A Mother's Teachings," 140-41; Camilla E. Kimball, "We Are His Children," 142-43

Temple

Gordon B. Hinckley, "A Great and Marvelous Statement," 69; Eugene England, "Welded Together in Spiritual Unity and Power and Beauty," 70; Spencer W. Kimball, "President Kimball Himself Played 'I Need Thee Every Hour'," 71

Temptation, Resistance to

Melvin J. Ballard, "Words of Comfort," 9-10; Boyd K. Packer, "The Inspiration of Sacred Music," 73; Spencer W. Kimball, "It Became a Part of My Life's Plan," 92-93; Lorin F. Wheelwright, "Our Parents Taught Us through Hymns," 108

Testimony

Yoshihiko Kikuchi, "The Upper Room," 5-6; Louisette

Castonguay, "Tears Started Flowing," 11; Alice Washburn, "Still Singing by My Side," 14; Jerry Borrowman, "You're the Future of the World," 27-28; Gordon B. Hinckley, "Praise to the Man," 102; David B. Haight, "In Humility, Our Savior," 105-6; Mary Johansen, "Love, from Your Daughter Barbara," 111-13

Therapy

Kathryn Wouden, "The Old Man Who Sang," 29-32

Understanding

Louisette Castonguay, "The Tears Started Flowing," 11

Word of Wisdom

Spencer W. Kimball, "In Our Lovely Deseret," 90-91; Spencer W. Kimball, "It Became a Part of My Life's Plan," 92-93; LeGrand Richards, "Who's on the Lord's Side?" 103-4

Worship

Joseph Walker, "The Hymns Are My Sermons," 76

Young, Brigham

Charles W. Penrose, "O Ye Mountains High," 44-45; LDS Missionary, "Saved by a Song," 154